# NATIONAL GEOGRAPHIC
# Reach
# for Reading

COMMON CORE PROGRAM

NATIONAL GEOGRAPHIC

Hampton-Brown

**Acknowledgments**

Grateful acknowledgment is given to the authors, artists, photographers, museums, publishers, and agents for permission to reprint copyrighted material. Every effort has been made to secure the appropriate permission. If any omissions have been made or if corrections are required, please contact the Publisher.

**Cover Illustration:** Joel Sotelo

**Cover Design and Art Direction:** Visual Asylum

**Illustration Credits:** All PM illustrations by National Geographic Learning.

Visit National Geographic Learning online at www.NGSP.com

Visit our corporate website at www.cengage.com

Printed in the USA.

Printer: RR Donnelley, Harrisonburg, VA

ISBN: 978-11338-99617

12 13 14 15 16 17 18 19 20 21

10 9 8 7 6 5 4 3 2 1

# Contents

## Unit 1: Hello, Neighbor!

# Unit 2: Staying Alive

# Unit 3: Water for Everyone

# Unit 4: Lend a Hand

Name _____ Date _____

# Short *a*

Circle the word that names the picture.

**1.**

cat      cot

**2.**

vat      van

**3.**

map      man

**4.**

hat      ham

**5.**

pan      pat

**6.**

mad      mat

**7.**

can      cab

**8.**

bag      bat

**9.**

fat      fan

**Read It Together**    Find a hat and a pan.

Name _____ Date _____

# Character

Make a character map for Jae and Vera from the song "Our Hometown Workers."

| Character | Who the Character Is | What the Character's Job Is |
|---|---|---|
|  |  |  |
|  |  |  |

💬 Share your character map with a partner.

Name _____  Date _____

# Short *a*

Write the word that completes each sentence.

**1. ran    cat**

I have a _____ .

**2. lap    tap**

The cat is on my _____ .

**3. hat    pat**

I like to _____ my cat.

**4. mat    van**

Dad is in the _____ .

**5. map    fat**

Dad has a _____ in the van.

**6. can    bat**

The map _____ help him.

**7. mat    ran**

Can you see the _____ ?

**8. rat    tan**

The mat is _____ .

**9. sat    yam**

Jan _____ on the mat.

**Phonics**

# Final -s

Write the word that completes each sentence.

**1. pal    pals**

Dad and Al are _____ .

**2. his    has**

Al _____ a van.

**3. is    as**

Al _____ in the van.

**4. cap    caps**

I see _____ in the van, too.

**5. find    finds**

Al _____ a tan cap!

**6. like    likes**

Dad _____ my tan cap.

**7. hat    hats**

Al and I find a _____ for Dad.

**8. is    his**

It _____ tan.

**9. as    has**

Dad _____ a tan hat, and I have a tan cap!

Name _____     Date _____

# High Frequency Words

Trace each High Frequency Word and then write it.

day day

there there

do do

what what

help help

by by

then then

people people

# Word Cards: Words with Short *a*, Final *-s*

| | | | |
|---|---|---|---|
| cat | bat | ax | van |
| maps | ham | man | hat |
| at | laps | ban | ran |
| Max | am | traps | dad |
| tax | mad | slaps | pan |
| fan | wax | yam | swam |
| back | caps | flat | sacks |

For use with TE p. T1j          **PM1.6**          **Unit 1** | Hello, Neighbor!

# High Frequency Word Cards

| | |
|---|---|
| I | see |
| too | what |
| have | help |
| a | people |
| the | do |
| my | there |
| is | by |
| on | day |
| it | then |

For use with TE p. T1j          **PM1.7**          **Unit 1** | Hello, Neighbor!

**Phonics**

# Short *i*

Circle the word that names the picture.

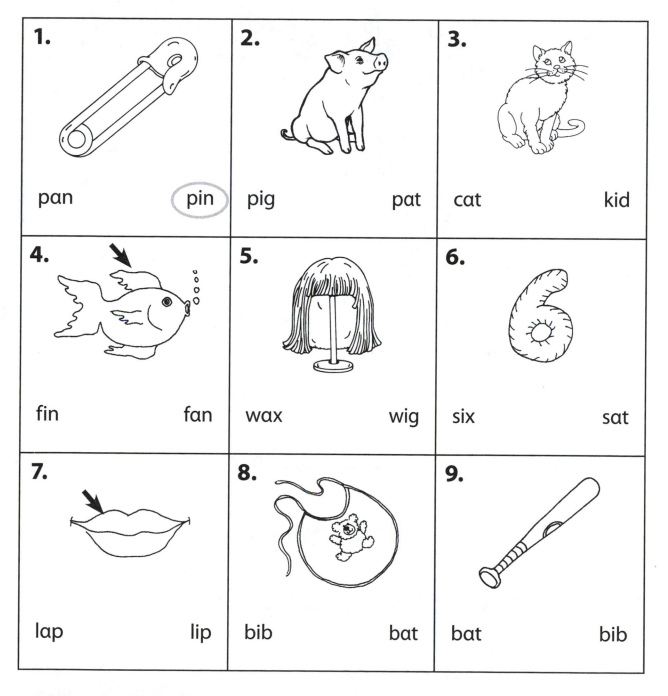

1. pan    (pin)

2. pig    pat

3. cat    kid

4. fin    fan

5. wax    wig

6. six    sat

7. lap    lip

8. bib    bat

9. bat    bib

**Read It Together**  Where is the pig? Where is the bib?

Name _____  Date _____

**High Frequency Words**

# Max and His Cat

Write a word from the box to complete each sentence.

| **High Frequency Words** |
| --- |
| by |
| day |
| do |
| help |
| people |
| then |
| there |
| what |

**1.** Max and his cat have a big _____ !

**2.** Max sees his cat go _____ him.

**3.** _____ Max cannot see his cat!

**4.** Where is his cat? It is up _____ !

**5.** _____ can Max do?

**6.** He can find _____ to help!

© National Geographic Learning, a part of Cengage Learning, Inc.
For use with TE p. T9d          **PM1.9**          **Unit 1** | Hello, Neighbor!

# Word Cards: Plural Nouns

| s | es | y | i + es |
|---|---|---|---|
| box | cat | church | glass |
| branch | library | lunch | farm |
| bush | town | park | dish |
| office | potato | community | place |
| home | hospital | city | school |
| store | address | sandwich | road |
| crash | pony | beach | walk |
| story | wind | berry | tree |

For use with TE p. T1m

**PM1.10**

**Phonics**

# Short *i*

Write the word that completes each sentence.

**1. six    sax**

I have _____ pigs.

**2. had    hid**

That pig _____ by the bin.

**3. did    dad**

I _____ find it there!

**4. hit    hat**

The little pig sat on my tan _____ !

**5. big    bag**

This pig is not little. It is _____ .

**6. pat    pit**

I like to _____ this pig.

**7. It    At**

_____ likes that!

**8. as    is**

That pig _____ not my pig.

**9. his    has**

It is _____ pig!

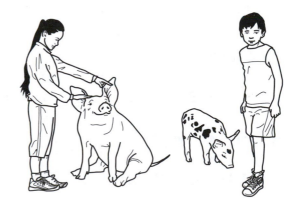

For use with TE p. T22a          **PM1.11**

Name _____ Date _____

# Possessives

**Write the word that completes each sentence.**

1. **Dan    Dan's**

   This is _____ cat.

2. **Pat    Pat's**

   The cat is in _____ hat.

3. **cat    cat's**

   The _____ naps in the hat!

4. **kids    kids'**

   I see the _____ cats, too.

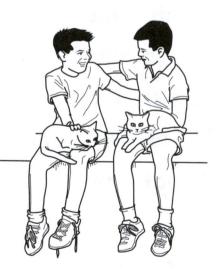

5. **pals    pals'**

   The cats are in the _____ laps.

6. **cats    cats'**

   The _____ nap in the laps.

7. **Dad    Dad's**

   Where is _____ cat?

8. **cats    cats'**

   It is not on the _____ mat.

9. **Kim    Kim's**

   It naps in _____ cap!

**Grammar and Writing**

# Write Plural Nouns

**Read the story. Then choose a word from the box that goes with each sentence and make it plural.**

| | | |
|---|---|---|
| glass | box | party |
| hat | game | hutch |

Last summer, I went to three __parties__. At

one party, we made a big fort out of cardboard

_____. We played fun _____ at every party.

At Robert's party, we drank apple juice out of cool

red _____. At Sarah's party, we got to take her pet

rabbits out of their _____. The thing I remember

most about Kareem's party is the crazy paper

_____ we wore.

Name _____  Date _____

# Quinito's Neighborhood

Make a character map for the people in "Quinito's Neighborhood."

| Character | Who the Character Is | What the Character's Job Is |
|---|---|---|
| Mami and Papi | Quinito's parents | She is a carpenter. He is a nurse. |
| Guillermo | Quinito's neighbor | |
| Dona Estrella | | She is a seamstress. |
| | | |

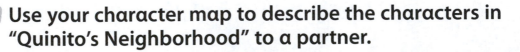 Use your character map to describe the characters in "Quinito's Neighborhood" to a partner.

**Phonics**

# Short *o*

Circle the word that names the picture.

| | | |
|---|---|---|
| **1.** bag   (box) | **2.** hot   hat | **3.** lot   log |
| **4.** fan   fox | **5.** tag   top | **6.** fox   fix |
| **7.** pot   pat | **8.** mop   man | **9.** dog   dig |

**Read It Together**   What can fit in a box?

Name _____ Date _____

# Short *o*

Write the word that completes each sentence.

**1. dig   dog**

Jax is my _____ .

**2. big   bog**

He is _____ and tan.

**3. jig   jog**

Jax and I like to _____ .

**4. log   lag**

We see a _____ by the bog.

**5. hat   hot**

Jax is _____ .

**6. hips   hops**

Jax _____ on the log.

**7. top   tap**

He sits on _____ .

**8. fix   fox**

Look! A _____ comes out!

**9. on   an**

Jax and I jog _____ !

Name _____     Date _____

# Syllables

Circle the word that names the picture.

| | | |
|---|---|---|
| **1.** pit / pig | **2.** cat / cot | **3.** dog / dig |
| **4.** six / sax | **5.** log / lot | **6.** mop / map |
| **7.** on / ox | **8.** fan / fin | **9.** wag / wig |
| **10.** pin / pan | **11.** ax / at | **12.** hot / hat |

**Read It Together**     A dog can dig. Can you dig, too?

**PM1.17**

Name _____    Date _____

# High Frequency Words

**Trace each High Frequency Word and then write it.**

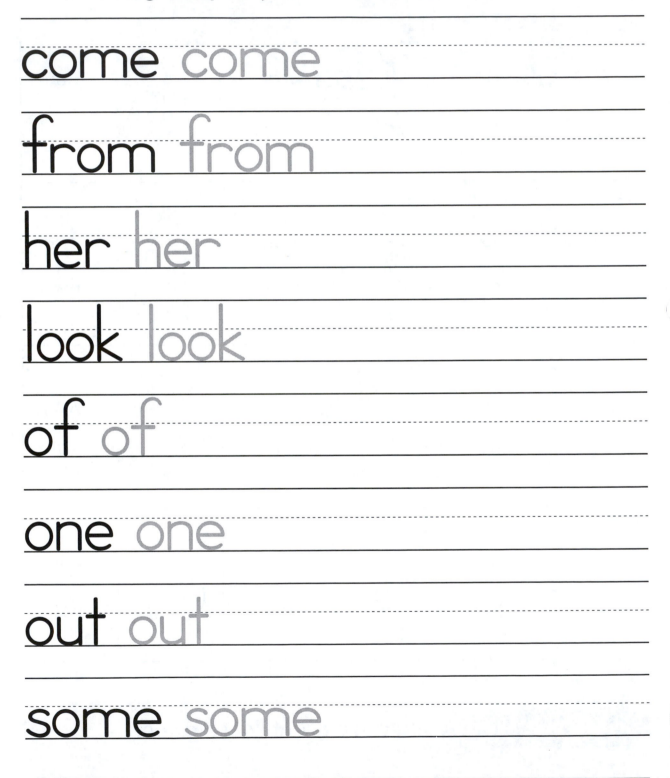

come come

from from

her her

look look

of of

one one

out out

some some

**PM1.18**

# Word Cards: Words with Short *o*

| | | | |
|---|---|---|---|
| lock | top | pot | cob |
| sob | mop | spot | dot |
| sock | con | Tom | job |
| flock | lot | hop | rob |
| rock | rot | blob | stop |
| lob | hot | pop | flop |
| cotton | dock | bottom | Ron |

**PM1.19**   Unit 1 | Hello, Neighbor!

# High Frequency Word Cards

| | |
|---|---|
| you | are |
| all | of |
| not | out |
| here | one |
| find | some |
| his | from |
| and | come |
| where | her |
| little | look |

For use with TE p. T25g

Unit 1 | Hello, Neighbor!

Name _____     Date _____

# Compare Genres

**Show how realistic fiction and a photo-essay are different.**

| Realistic Fiction | Photo-Essay |
|---|---|
| • tells about things that could really happen | • uses photographs and text to tell about a topic |

**Take turns with a partner. Give information about a story or a photo-essay.**

For use with TE p. T29h                    **PM1.21**                    Unit 1 | Hello, Neighbor!

Name _____ Date _____

# Syllable Division

Divide each word into syllables. Circle the word that names the picture.

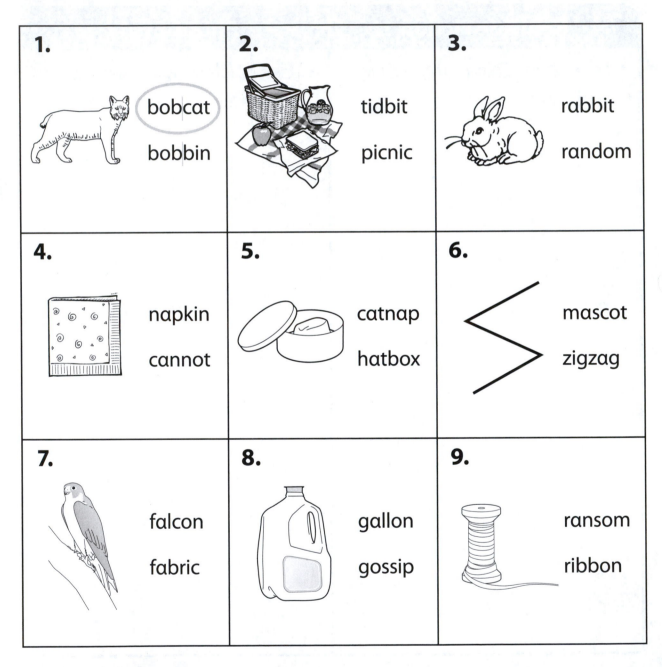

**1.** bobcat / bobbin

**2.** tidbit / picnic

**3.** rabbit / random

**4.** napkin / cannot

**5.** catnap / hatbox

**6.** mascot / zigzag

**7.** falcon / fabric

**8.** gallon / gossip

**9.** ransom / ribbon

**Read It Together** Do you see a bobcat or a napkin at a picnic?

**High Frequency Words**

# Hats in a Box

Write a word from the box to complete each sentence.

| High Frequency **Words** |
|---|
| come |
| from |
| her |
| look |
| of |
| one |
| out |
| some |

1. Jan got this hatbox _____ her attic.

2. Come _____ at it.

3. There are _____ hats in the box!

4. _____ hat has ribbons.

5. A lot _____ the ribbons are big!

6. Look! That hat is _____ of the box and on Jan!

For use with TE p. T30d     **PM1.23**     Unit 1 | Hello, Neighbor!

Name _____ Date _____

# Use Plural Nouns

1. Take turns with a partner.

2. Toss a marker onto the game board.

3. Follow the directions in the square you land on.

4. After you say your sentence, your partner says a sentence with a different noun of the same type.

| | |
|---|---|
| Say a sentence with a plural noun that ends in **s**. | Say a sentence with a plural noun that changes its spelling. |
| Say a sentence with a plural noun that ends in **es**. | Say a sentence with a plural noun that does not change its form. |
| Say a sentence with a plural noun that ends in **ies**. | Say a sentence with a collective noun. |

Name _____ Date _____

# Syllable Division

Divide the words into syllables. Write the word that completes each sentence.

**1. picnic    gallon**

Mom, Dad, Ron, and Ron's dog are on a _____ .

**2. canyon    catnap**

Ron's dog, Sam, had a _____ . Then he got up.

**3. cannot    bobcat**

Sam _____ sit. He digs!

**4. napkin    attic**

He digs up one _____ .

**5. zigzag    ribbon**

He digs up some _____ .

**6. admit    fabric**

He finds some tan _____ , too.

**7. fossil    gossip**

Look! Sam digs up a _____ !

**8. gallon    rabbit**

It is not from a _____ .

**9. tidbit    bobcat**

It is from a _____ !

# Write Plural and Collective Nouns

**Read the story. Then choose a word from the box that goes with each sentence and make it plural if necessary.**

| | | |
|---|---|---|
| lunch | baby | fish |
| man | family | park |

Our neighborhood has two great ____parks____

kids can play in. One park has a big pond. You can

see lots of moms and dads there pushing their new

_____ in strollers. They like to look at the _____

that swim in the pond. One _____ had a picnic

on Saturday. The parents and kids ate their _____

sitting under a big maple tree. After they left, two

_____ sat under the tree and played guitars.

**Grammar: Plural Nouns**

# Say Plural Nouns

1. Play with a partner.

2. Spin the spinner.

3. Change the noun to a plural noun.

4. Say a sentence using the plural noun.

**Make a Spinner**

1. Put a paper clip ⬭ in the center of the circle.

2. Hold one end of the paper clip with a pencil.

3. Spin the paper clip around the pencil.

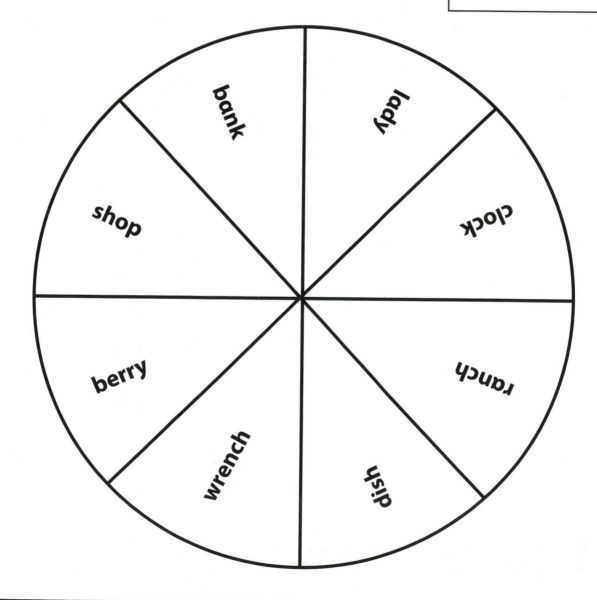

**Phonics**

# Short e

**Circle the word that names the picture.**

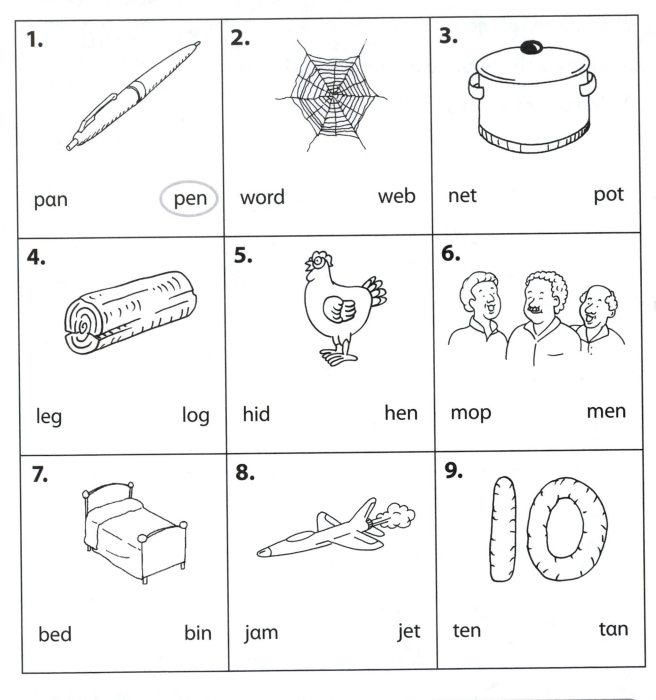

1. pan    (pen)

2. word    web

3. net    pot

4. leg    log

5. hid    hen

6. mop    men

7. bed    bin

8. jam    jet

9. ten    tan

**Read It Together**    Ten men get the ten jets.

**Details Cluster**

# Our Community

Make a details cluster to tell about places in your community.

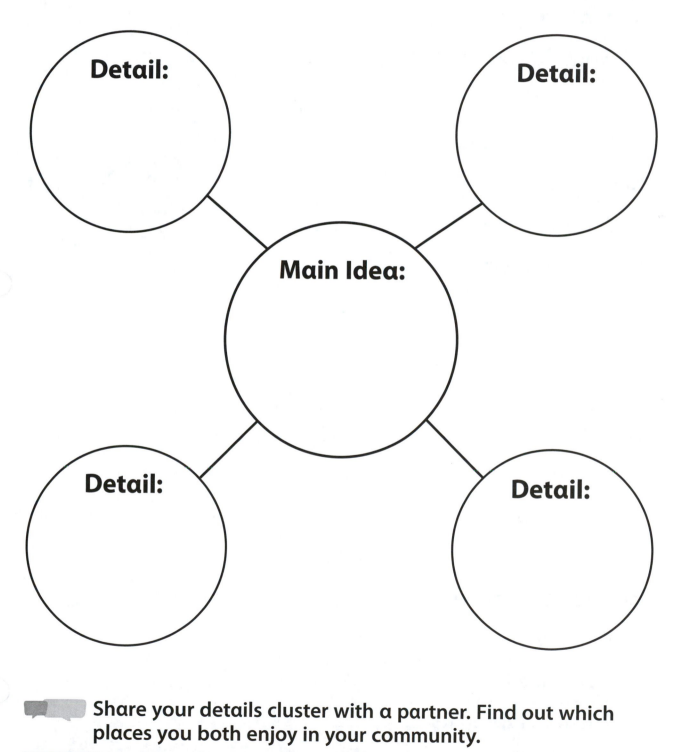

Share your details cluster with a partner. Find out which places you both enjoy in your community.

Phonics

# Short *e*

Write the word that completes each sentence.

**1. den    din**

What do you see come out of its _____ ?

**2. rid    red**

It is a _____ fox.

**3. pat    pet**

This fox is not a _____ .

**4. hen    happen**

The fox sees your _____ .

**5. lot    let**

Do not _____ the fox get it!

**6. legs    lags**

The fox jogs fast on its _____ .

**7. Tin    Then**

_____ it finds its den.

**8. happen    hectic**

What will _____ here?

**9. bad    bed**

The fox naps in its _____ !

**Handwriting**

# High Frequency Words

Trace each High Frequency Word and then write it.

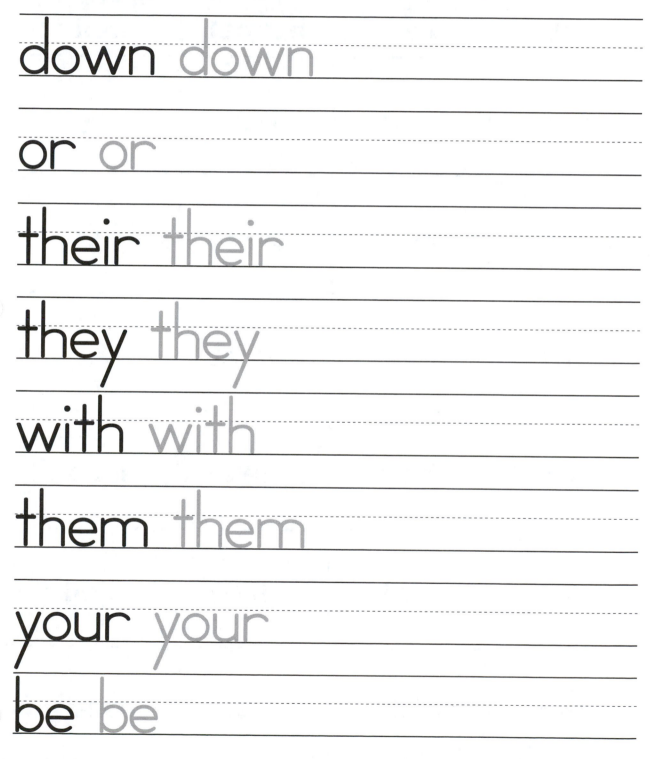

down down

or or

their their

they they

with with

them them

your your

be be

For use with TE p. T34f

**PM1.31**

# Word Cards: Words with short *e*

| | | | |
|---|---|---|---|
| jet | hen | helmet | bell |
| vet | nest | bet | beg |
| sell | men | peg | pet |
| tell | best | forget | set |
| red | help | bell | lend |
| rest | yell | den | send |
| ten | fell | test | end |

For use with TE p. T31i    **PM1.32**    **Unit 1** | Hello, Neighbor!

# High Frequency Word Cards

| am | as |
|----|----|
| him | with |
| for | their |
| at | be |
| go | them |
| to | your |
| we | down |
| has | they |
| she | or |

For use with TE p. T31i  **PM1.33**  Unit 1 | Hello, Neighbor!

**Phonics**

# Short *u*

Circle the word that names the picture.

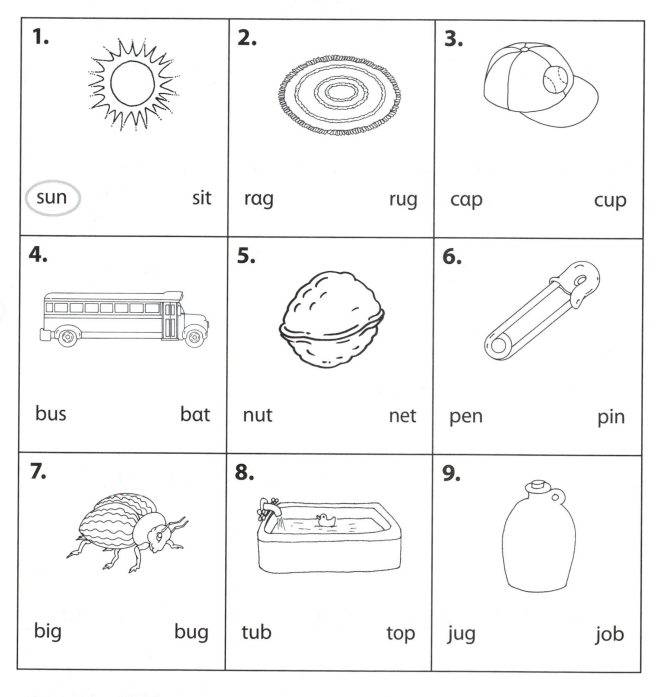

1.
sun                    sit

2.
rag                    rug

3.
cap                    cup

4.
bus                    bat

5.
nut                    net

6.
pen                    pin

7.
big                    bug

8.
tub                    top

9.
jug                    job

**Read It Together**   What bugs do you like?

Name _____ Date _____

# Kittens in a Basket

Write a word from the box to complete each sentence.

1. What is in _____ basket?

2. I have kittens. Look down, and you can

   see _____ .

3. Look at _____ legs.

   They look like mittens!

4. It can _____ fun to have a kitten. Can I

   get one?

5. You can have the big kitten _____ the

   little one.

6. You can have fun _____ your kitten.

| High Frequency Words |
| --- |
| be |
| down |
| or |
| their |
| them |
| they |
| with |
| your |

**Grammar: Proper Nouns**

# Use Proper Nouns

1. Take turns with a partner.

2. Toss a marker onto the game board.

3. Follow the directions in the square you land on.

| | | |
|---|---|---|
| Say a sentence with a **day of the week**. | Say a sentence with a **month**. | Say a sentence with a **holiday**. |
| Say a sentence with a **day of the week**. | Say a sentence with a **proper noun that names a special date**. | Say a sentence with a **holiday**. |
| Say a sentence with **two different days of the week**. | Say a sentence with **two different months**. | Say a sentence with **two different holidays**. |

**Phonics**

# Short *u*

**Write the word that completes each sentence.**

1. **up    an**

   The sun comes _____ , and Gus gets out of bed.

2. **mud    muffin**

   He gets a _____ . Yum!

3. **nets    nuts**

   It has _____ in it. Yum! Yum!

4. **jogs    jugs**

   Gus _____ with his pal Jed.

5. **us    until**

   They run _____ ten.

6. **hut    hot**

   Then the sun gets too _____ .

7. **fun    fan**

   The pals get wet and have _____ .

8. **sat    sunset**

   Gus sees the sun go down. He likes the _____ .

9. **bed    bud**

   Gus is in his _____ . He had a fun day!

**Grammar and Writing**

# Write Proper Nouns

**Read the story. Then choose a word from the box that goes with each sentence.**

| | | |
|---|---|---|
| September | Fourth of July | Peterson Fireworks Company |
| Mrs. Minh | Oak Street | Saturday |

Brandon was walking down _____Oak Street_____. It was

a sunny _____ morning in _____. Up on

the next block he saw lots of flashing lights. *Hmm*, he

thought, *it looks like the fireworks on the* _____.

Brandon crossed the street and walked up to the next

block. There he saw a bunch of fire engines and police

cars. He saw his neighbor _____ looking at a

building. She waved to Brandon and then pointed at

_____. The building was on fire! *It*

*really is like Independence Day*, thought Brandon.

**Vocabulary**

# Vocabulary Bingo

1. Write one Key Word in each building.

2. Listen to the clues. Find the Key Word and use a marker to cover it.

3. Say "Bingo" when you have four markers in a row.

| Key Words | |
|---|---|
| area | locate |
| building | park |
| home | place |
| hospital | population |
| identify | school |
| library | |

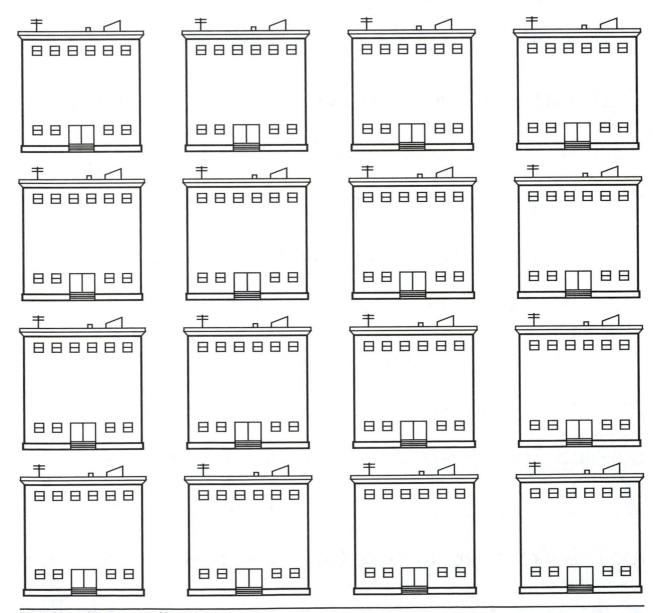

Name _____  Date _____

# Be My Neighbor

Make a details cluster for "Be My Neighbor." Look for details that tell more about the main idea.

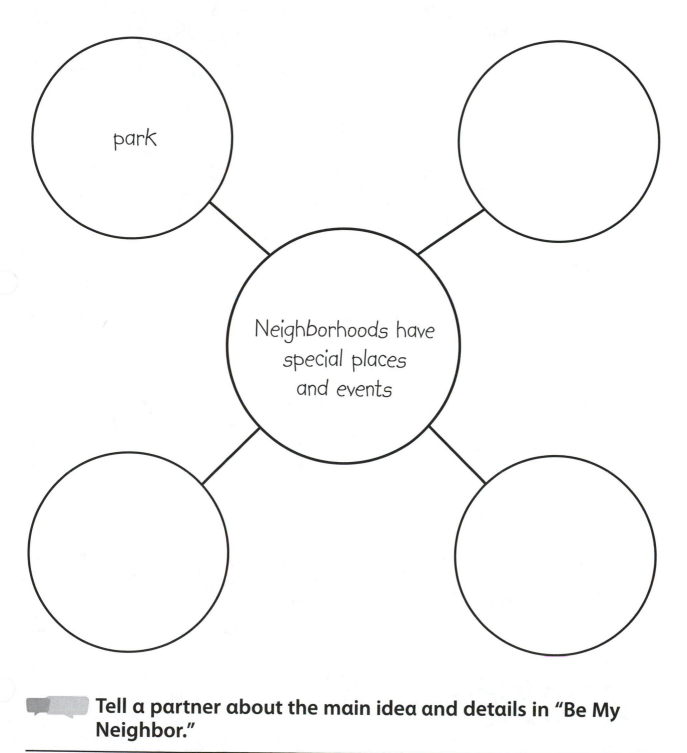

💬 **Tell a partner about the main idea and details in "Be My Neighbor."**

**Phonics**

# Consonants *ck, ng*

Circle the word that names the picture.

**1.**
dug
(duck)
dud

**2.**
song
sob
sock

**3.**
lick
lock
long

**4.**
rabbit
rocket
robs

**5.**
lock
lots
long

**6.**
sit
sick
sing

**7.**
tang
tag
tack

**8.**
jack
jacket
jam

**9.**
king
kin
kitten

**10.**
kick
kit
kiss

**11.**
wick
wing
wins

**12.**
rang
rock
rots

**Read It Together**  The king with a ring can sing!

**Phonics**

# Consonants *ck, ng*

Write the word that completes each sentence.

1. **King   Kick**

   _____ Nick is sad.

2. **ring   rips**

   He cannot find his red _____ .

3. **jogs   jacket**

   He finds his red _____ .

4. **people   pocket**

   He looks in the _____ .

5. **song   sock**

   He finds a tan _____ with zigzags.

6. **pack   pang**

   He finds a _____ of gum, too.

7. **dug   duck**

   Then Nick sees his pet _____ .

8. **wing   wick**

   The duck has Nick's ring on his _____ .

9. **lock   long**

   Nick is not sad! He sings a _____ song!

**Phonics**

# Double Consonants

**Write the word to complete each sentence.**

**1. hiss   hill**

Jack and Jill go up a _____ .

**2. pass   pack**

They _____ a big log.

**3. mock   moss**

It has _____ on it.

**4. eggs   adds**

The pals sit down to have some _____ .

**5. mill   mess**

They make a _____ .

**6. buzz   buck**

Some bugs come out and _____ by.

**7. ill   off**

Jack and Jill hop _____ that log!

**8. will   wing**

What _____ they do?

**9. huff   hull        putt   puff**

They _____ and _____ and run back down!

**Handwriting**

# High Frequency Words

**Trace each High Frequency Word and then write it.**

each each

no no

said said

saw saw

use use

was was

were were

who who

# Word Cards: Words with -*ck*, -*ng*

| sock | truck | string | building |
|------|-------|--------|----------|
| black | duck | hung | trick |
| tackle | ring | fling | quick |
| hang | bang | slick | tickle |
| sing | thing | strong | rung |
| lock | flock | rock | song |
| lick | sung | long | nick |

For use with TE p. T53g          **PM1.45**          **Unit 1** | Hello, Neighbor!

# High Frequency Word Cards

| | |
|---|---|
| like | when |
| but | said |
| so | no |
| this | use |
| if | was |
| that | were |
| he | saw |
| in | each |
| up | who |

For use with TE p. T53g      **PM1.46**      **Unit 1** | Hello, Neighbor!

Name _____ Date _____

# Compare Media

Use this chart to compare "Be My Neighbor" and "My Favorite Place."

| | Photo-Essay | Internet Bulletin Board |
|---|---|---|
| has photos | ✓ | ✓ |
| has captions | | |
| has more than one writer | | |
| gives facts | | |
| asks and answers questions | | |
| lets people share ideas and communicate | | |

Take turns with a partner. Ask each other questions about a photo-essay or an Internet bulletin board.

**Phonics**

# Short Vowels

### Circle the word that names the picture.

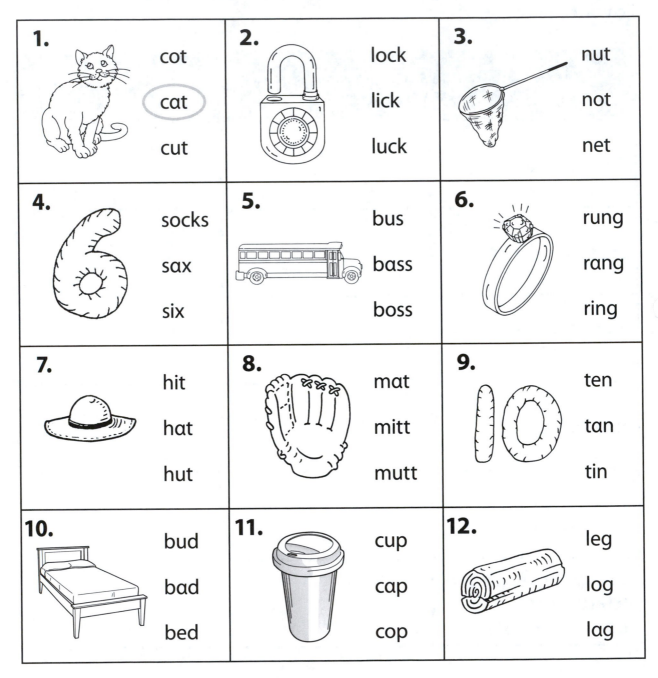

1. cot
   (cat)
   cut

2. lock
   lick
   luck

3. nut
   not
   net

4. socks
   sax
   six

5. bus
   bass
   boss

6. rung
   rang
   ring

7. hit
   hat
   hut

8. mat
   mitt
   mutt

9. ten
   tan
   tin

10. bud
    bad
    bed

11. cup
    cap
    cop

12. leg
    log
    lag

**Read It Together**   I see six socks and a sax!

# What Did We See?

**Write a word from the box to complete each sentence.**

| High Frequency Words |
| --- |
| each |
| no |
| said |
| saw |
| use |
| was |
| where |
| who |

1. Matt said, "Can you tell what my pals

   _____

   _____ pass by?".

2. Ming said, "They _____ little."

3. Mack said, "Was _____ one tan?"

4. Pam said, "_____. One was tan."

5. Lin said, "They _____ their legs to hop."

6. Matt said, "What did my pals see? _____

   can tell us?"

# Word Cards

| | , | s | |
|---|---|---|---|
| house | street | neighborhood | friends |
| Mom | Dad | Grandmother | Grandfather |
| dogs | birds | trees | leaves |
| cars | trucks | sidewalk | park |
| ponds | bugs | zoo | animals |
| buildings | bus | trains | schools |
| playground | stores | bridge | Mr. Flores |
| Mrs. Brown | Dr. Adams | Capt. Smith | policewoman |

For use with TE p. T53j      **PM1.50**      Unit 1 | Hello, Neighbor!

Name _____ Date _____

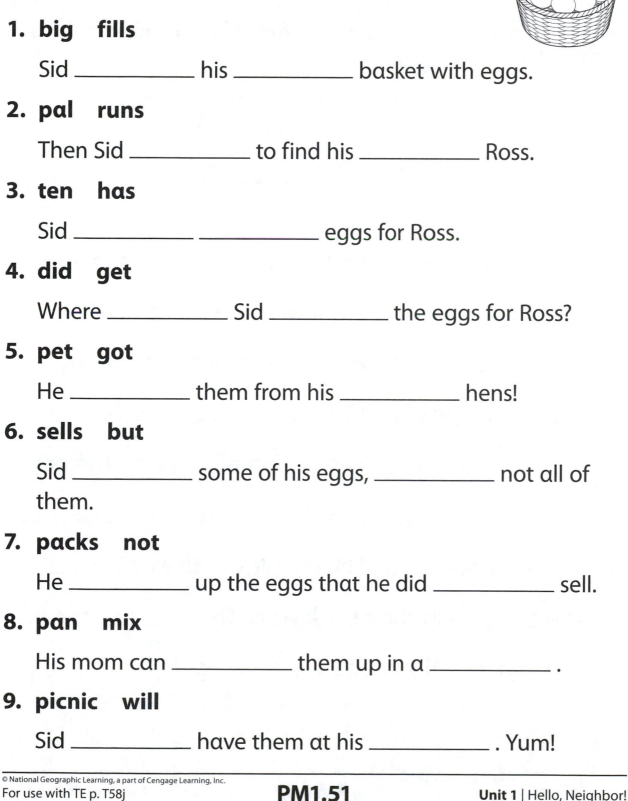

# Short Vowels

Write the words to complete each sentence.

**1. big    fills**

Sid _____ his _____ basket with eggs.

**2. pal    runs**

Then Sid _____ to find his _____ Ross.

**3. ten    has**

Sid _____ _____ eggs for Ross.

**4. did    get**

Where _____ Sid _____ the eggs for Ross?

**5. pet    got**

He _____ them from his _____ hens!

**6. sells    but**

Sid _____ some of his eggs, _____ not all of them.

**7. packs    not**

He _____ up the eggs that he did _____ sell.

**8. pan    mix**

His mom can _____ them up in a _____ .

**9. picnic    will**

Sid _____ have them at his _____ . Yum!

Grammar and Writing

# Write Possessive Nouns and Abbreviations

**Read the story. Then choose a word from the box that goes with each sentence.**

| Mr. | Jason's | Ling's |
|-----|---------|--------|
| sister's | puppies' | neighbors' |

I really like my neighborhood. Some of my _neighbors'_ homes are big and some are small. My friend _____ house is across the street. It's big because he has eight brothers and sisters. My _____ boyfriend lives in a little house on the next block. He plays soccer with me sometimes. _____ Ling lives next door. I like to play with Mrs. _____ new puppies in their back yard. The _____ fur is very soft, but their tongues are rough!

Name _____ Date _____

# Use Proper and Possessive Nouns

> ## Grammar Rules  Proper and Possessive Nouns
>
> - A proper noun names a specific person, place, or thing. (Example: Texas)
>
> - Some titles of people begin with a capital letter and end with a period. (Example: Dr.)
>
> - A possessive noun names an owner. (Example: Jackson's)

**Underline the proper nouns and write them in the chart. Then make each proper noun possessive. The first one is done for you.**

<u>Mrs. Preston</u> lives in a neighborhood called Grandview. Her home is on Maple Street. Adam Preston is her son. We go to the same school. He is on my soccer team, too. Mr. Mohr is our coach.

| Proper Nouns | Proper Possessive Nouns |
|---|---|
| Mrs. Preston | Mrs. Preston's |
|  |  |
|  |  |
|  |  |

**Write a sentence with a proper noun and a proper possessive noun. Read your sentence to a partner.**

**Phonics**

# Blends with *r, l*

Circle the word that names the picture.

1. tag
   (flag)
   drag

2. plug
   slug
   jug

3. class
   glass
   grass

4. drum
   plum
   hum

5. log
   clog
   frog

6. truck
   cluck
   pluck

7. flap
   trap
   clap

8. bricks
   tricks
   flicks

9. slab
   crab
   lab

10. frock
    block
    clock

11. grin
    win
    bring

12. drill
    flannel
    pretzel

**Read It Together**   Grin and clap if you like pretzels.

Name _____  Date _____

**Beginning-Middle-End Chart**

# The Nature Walk

Make a story map to tell about a nature walk.

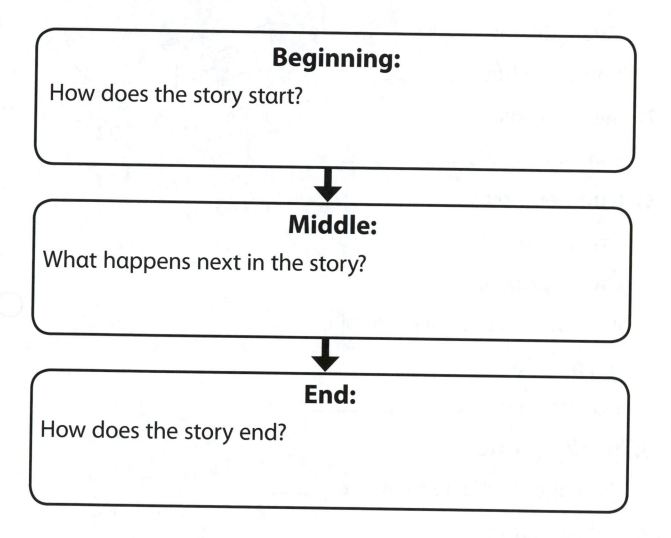

**Beginning:**
How does the story start?

**Middle:**
What happens next in the story?

**End:**
How does the story end?

**Share your Beginning-Middle-End Chart with your partner.**

Name _____  Date _____

# Blends with *r, l*

Write the word that completes each sentence.

**1. plus    drums**

Tran's dad has _____.

**2. bless    brass**

Some of them are _____.

**3. trumpet    trot**

Tran has a _____.

**4. click    plastic**

It is not _____. It is brass!

**5. bran    plan**

Dad and Tran have a _____.

**6. truck    pluck**

Tran and Dad get into the red _____.

**7. bring    cling**

They _____ their drums and trumpet.

**8. glass    class**

Then they go to Tran's _____.

**9. trap    clap**

All of Tran's pals _____.

**Handwriting**

# High Frequency Words

Trace each High Frequency Word and then write it.

these these

body body

back back

how how

eat eat

those those

way way

into into

# Word Cards: Blends with *r, l*

| | | | |
|---|---|---|---|
| flag | brick | clock | truck |
| flatten | plastic | trick | problem |
| black | grip | block | trap |
| dragon | frantic | click | slap |
| traffic | grass | slid | glad |
| crab | plan | printed | glob |
| blast | drop | slip | cracking |

© National Geographic Learning, a part of Cengage Learning, Inc.
For use with TE p. T65k  **PM2.5**

# High Frequency Word Cards

| | |
|---|---|
| what | way |
| help | back |
| people | eat |
| do | those |
| there | how |
| by | into |
| day | these |
| then | body |

For use with TE p. T65k

**PM2.6**

Unit 2 | Staying Alive

Name _____ Date _____

# Blends with *s*

Circle the word that names the picture.

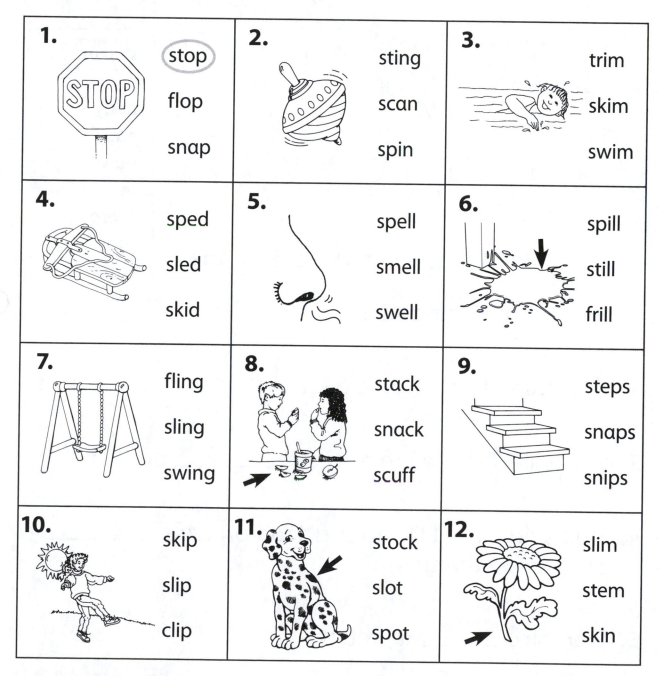

**1.** stop / flop / snap

**2.** sting / scan / spin

**3.** trim / skim / swim

**4.** sped / sled / skid

**5.** spell / smell / swell

**6.** spill / still / frill

**7.** fling / sling / swing

**8.** stack / snack / scuff

**9.** steps / snaps / snips

**10.** skip / slip / clip

**11.** stock / slot / spot

**12.** slim / stem / skin

**Read It Together**   Do you like to swim, skip, or swing?

**High Frequency Words**

# A Pack of Pretzels

**Write a word from the box to complete each sentence.**

| High Frequency **Words** |
| --- |
| back |
| body |
| eat |
| how |
| into |
| these |
| those |
| way |

**1.** Fran said, "What is in that pack on the

_____ of your body?"

**2.** Fred said, "Look. I have a lot of stuff to _____ in it."

**3.** Fran said, "These are nuts. Are _____ pretzels?"

**4.** Fred said, "Yes. I like to snack on pretzels." _____
do you like them?

**5.** Fran bit _____ a pretzel.

**6.** Fran said, "I like them a lot! I will find a _____ to
get pretzels, too!"

Name _____     Date _____

# Build Sentences

Cut out the cards and make a gray pile with the cards facedown. Spread out the white cards face up. Pick one gray card. Then choose a white card that matches the gray card you picked. Say a sentence using the word on the gray card and the word on the white card. Then put the cards on the bottom of the piles.

| can | might | do | does |
|---|---|---|---|
| fly | eat | think | run |
| hold | wish | drink | play |
| hear | see | taste | listen |
| walk | swim | imagine | touch |

**Phonics**

# Blends with *s*

Write the word that completes each sentence.

1.  **stiff    sniff**

    The dogs _____ in the grass.

2.  **stick    slick**

    One dog finds a _____ in the grass.

3.  **slot    spot**

    One dog finds a _____ in the sun and naps.

4.  **smell    swell**

    One dog sniffs. What can it _____?

5.  **slug    snug**

    It smells a fox that is _____ in its den.

6.  **slop    stop**

    Then the fox runs and will not _____.

7.  **still    squid**

    The dog is _____, but looks at the fox.

8.  **spill    speck**

    The fox runs until it is a little _____.

9.  **scans    stacks**

    The dog _____ the grass. It cannot see the fox.

**Phonics**

# Triple Blends with *s*

Circle the word that names the picture.

1.
spot
stick
(split)

2.
scraps
stacks
skips

3.
sting
spring
sling

4.
swing
string
sprig

5.
scrub
stub
scab

6.
splat
slat
scat

7.
scram
slum
strum

8.
snap
sap
strap

9.
sprig
swig
strung

10.
sprung
strong
scrod

11.
sprang
stuck
struck

12.
scruff
stuff
snuff

**Read It Together**   The strong dog springs up, eats scraps, and scrams!

Name _____  Date _____

# Write Action and Helping Verbs

Read the story. Then choose a word from the box that goes with each sentence.

| | | |
|---|---|---|
| carries | can fly | might sit |
| spot | sees | peep |

An owl _____*can fly*_____ without making any

noise. This bird also _____ very well in the

dark. A hunting owl _____ on a tree branch

to look and listen for small animals. Hungry baby

owls _____ impatiently for food. After

catching its dinner, the owl _____ it back to

its nest. If you _____ an owl, you have been

very lucky!

# Twilight Hunt

**Make a Beginning-Middle-End Chart to show the plot of "Twilight Hunt."**

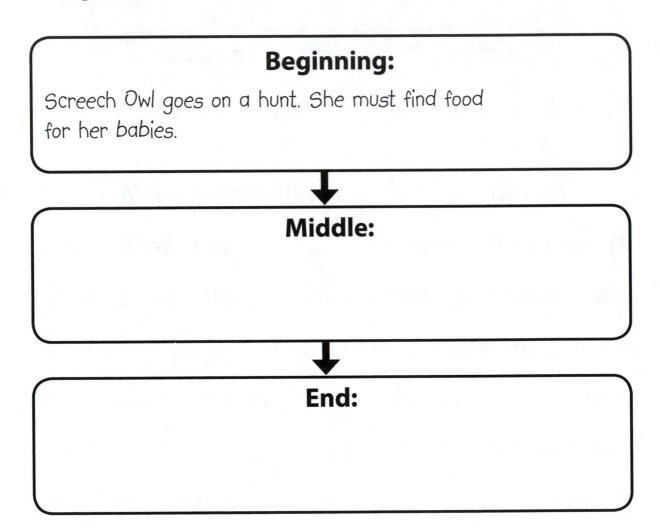

**Beginning:**

Screech Owl goes on a hunt. She must find food for her babies.

**Middle:**

**End:**

💬 **Use your Beginning-Middle-End Chart to tell your partner about "Twilight Hunt."**

Name _____  Date _____

# Final Blends

Circle the word that names the picture.

| 1. | plot<br>(plant)<br>plan | 2. | hand<br>hack<br>hang | 3. | skin<br>skit<br>skunk |
|---|---|---|---|---|---|
| 4. | nest<br>net<br>neck | 5. | best<br>bent<br>belt | 6. | lamp<br>land<br>lack |
| 7. | rang<br>raft<br>ramp | 8. | deck<br>dent<br>desk | 9. | test<br>tent<br>tell |
| 10. | bank<br>bang<br>band | 11. | vent<br>vend<br>vest | 12. | stamp<br>stack<br>stand |

**Read It Together**  Do you camp in a desk, a bank, or a tent?

**Phonics**

# Final Blends

**Write the word that completes each sentence.**

**1. pot   pond**

Trent just got to the _____.

**2. jump   just**

He will sprint down, _____ in, and get wet!

**3. pant   past**

Trent swims _____ plants and frogs.

**4. drink   drift**

Then Trent comes out and gets a _____.

**5. gulp   gust**

He likes to _____ it down fast.

**6. sand   sang**

Trent digs in the _____ for the rest of the day.

**7. song   soft**

The sand is _____ when it is wet.

**8. cast   camp**

Trent, his mom, and his dad _____ at the pond.

**9. tent   test**

At the end of the day, they go into their _____.

Name _____ Date _____

# High Frequency Words

**Trace each High Frequency Word and then write it.**

could could

good good

hard hard

now now

over over

part part

under under

very very

For use with TE p. T97b    **PM2.16**    **Unit 2** | Staying Alive

# Word Cards: Final Blends

| | | | |
|---|---|---|---|
| plant | jump | hand | trunk |
| hunt | must | slant | fond |
| wind | insect | trust | connect |
| help | blend | blank | plump |
| bank | think | lost | stamp |
| drink | subtract | gulp | clamp |
| stand | pink | stunt | fact |

# High Frequency Word Cards

| | |
|---|---|
| of | now |
| out | over |
| one | under |
| some | very |
| from | could |
| come | good |
| her | part |
| look | hard |

For use with TE p. T91g      **PM2.18**      Unit 2 | Staying Alive

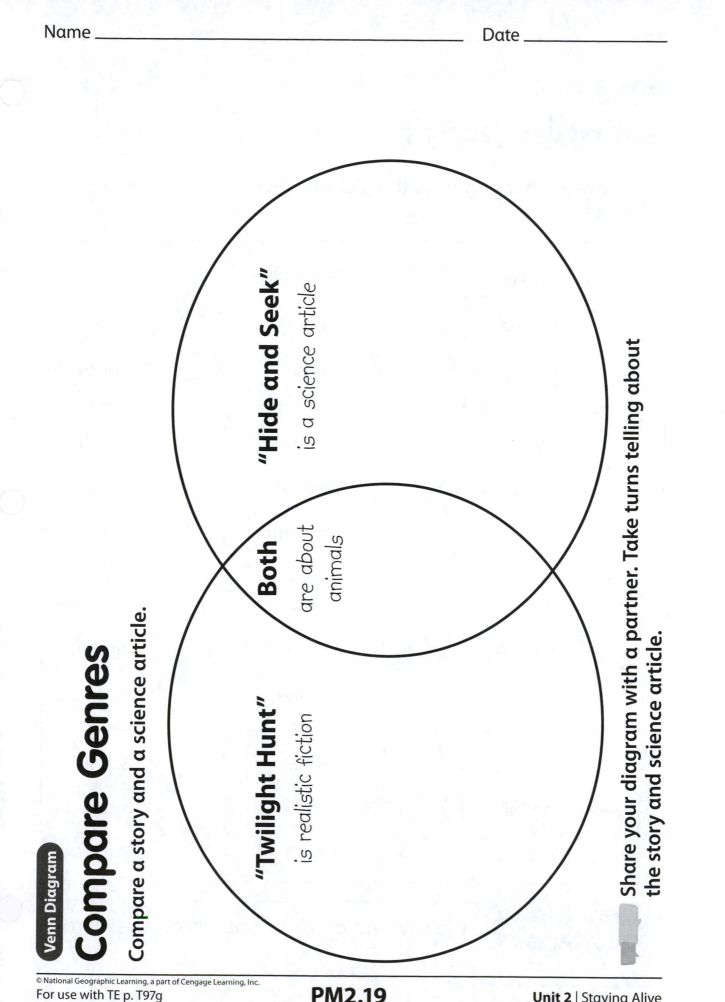

**Venn Diagram**

# Compare Genres

Compare a story and a science article.

**"Hide and Seek"**
is a science article

**Both**
are about animals

**"Twilight Hunt"**
is realistic fiction

Share your diagram with a partner. Take turns telling about the story and science article.

Name _____ Date _____

**Phonics**

# Syllable Division

Circle the word that names the picture. Divide the word into syllables.

| | | |
|---|---|---|
| **1.** basket / bobsled / (backpack) | **2.** drumsticks / ducklings / dentists | **3.** pumpkin / public / puppet |
| **4.** witness / windmill / wisdom | **5.** mattress / mistrust / manhunt | **6.** handbag / happen / napkin |
| **7.** hiccup / himself / hilltop | **8.** 100 — husband / helmet / hundred | **9.** sandbox / sapling / sadness |
| **10.** actress / anthill / attack | **11.** address / album / attract | **12.** 10 − 7 — subset / subject / subtract |

**Read It Together**  We saw hundreds of anthills on the hilltop.

# Find the Backpack!

Write a word from the box to complete each sentence.

| High Frequency Words |
|---|
| could |
| good |
| hard |
| now |
| over |
| part |
| under |
| very |

**1.** Where _____ my backpack be?

**2.** It is _____ hard to find! Can you help me?

**3.** It is not _____ my bed or over my bed.

**4.** It is not on my desk! Where can I look _____?

**5.** Look at my jacket! I see a strap under it! Is the strap

_____ of my backpack?

**6.** It is _____ that I have my backpack. Now where are my mittens?

Name _____    Date _____

# Use Helping Verbs

**Directions:**

1. Make a spinner.

2. Play with a partner.

3. Take turns spinning the spinner.

4. Read the word you land on. Say a sentence using **can, might, do,** or **does.** Then have your partner say another sentence using the same helping verb and a different main verb.

---

**Make a Spinner**

1. Put a paper clip 🔗 in the center of the circle.

2. Hold one end of the paper clip with a pencil.

3. Spin the paper clip around the pencil.

---

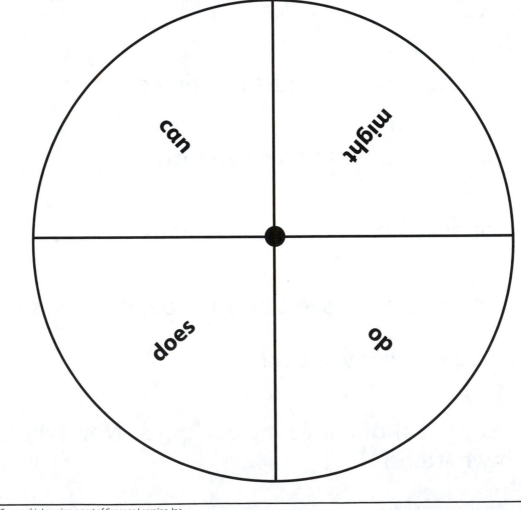

**Phonics**

# Syllable Division

**Divide the words into syllables. Then write the word that completes each sentence.**

**1. hilltop    tantrum**

Bess and Kent jog up to the _____.

**2. instant    anthill**

What do they see? Bess sees an _____!

**3. dentist    inspects**

Bess looks down and _____ it.

**4. address    hundreds**

She sees _____ of ants.

**5. ducklings    subtracts**

Kent sees six _____ in a pond.

**6. handful    grandpa**

Then Bess and Kent see their _____.

**7. backpack    tundra**

He gets a snack from his _____.

**8. pumpkin    napkin**

The snack is _____ muffins.

**9. helmets    gumdrops**

They eat muffins with _____ on top!

Name _____ Date _____

# Write Helping and Action Verbs

**Read the story. Choose a word from the box that goes with each sentence.**

| can | do | does |
|-----|-----|-----|
| hide | look | might |

Some animals can __hide__ themselves to stay

safe. An insect _____ use color or shape to hide

from its enemies. A mantis really _____ depend on

its green color and leaf shape to hide. A little red fish

does _____ exactly like the plants around it! Some

birds _____ blend in with the trees and flowers

around them. If I look on leaves carefully, I _____

find a mantis or a katydid.

**Grammar: Action and Helping Verbs**

# Roll a Verb

## Grammar Rules  Action and Helping Verbs

**For Action Verbs**
- Use **-s** at the end of an action verb if the subject is **he**, **she**, or **it**.
- Do not use **-s** for **I**, **you**, **we**, or **they**.

**For Action Verbs with Helping Verbs**
- A **helping verb** comes before the **main verb**.

Use a numbered game cube to play this game.

1. Roll the game cube. Find the helping verb that goes with the number.

2. Roll the game cube again. Find the action verb that goes with the number.

3. Say a sentence with the action verb and helping verb. The first player to use all six action verbs and helping verbs in sentences correctly wins.

| Helping Verbs | Action Verbs |
|---------------|--------------|
| 1.  do        | 1.  look     |
| 2.  does      | 2.  escape   |
| 3.  can       | 3.  fly      |
| 4.  might     | 4.  run      |
| 5.  do        | 5.  search   |
| 6.  can       | 6.  hide     |

**Phonics**

# Words with *ch, tch*

Circle the word that names the picture.

**1.**
(chick)
brick
quick

**2.**
camp
catch
cast

**3.**
past
pack
patch

**4.**
flunk
chunk
skunk

**5.**
branch
hatch
brand

**6.**
chin
grin
spin

**7.**
match
mast
mask

**8.**
drums
strums
chums

**9.**
crank
crutch
crust

**10.**
fleck
speck
check

**11.**
sandwich
sapling
such

**12.**
object
ostrich
chimp

**Read It Together**   Chuck and his chums scratch their chins.

Name _____   Date _____

# Creature Features

Compare animals and their features.

| Features | Creature 1 | Creature 2 |
|---|---|---|
|  |  |  |
|  |  |  |
|  |  |  |
|  |  |  |
|  |  |  |

Tell a partner how the animals are alike.

**Phonics**

# Words with *ch, tch*

Write the word that completes each sentence.

**1. chipmunk    trunk**

A little _____ collects nuts.

**2. chunk    lunch**

Will it eat the nuts for its _____?

**3. children    munch**

I like to _____ on nuts, too!

**4. chimp    catch**

A big _____ eats some nuts.

**5. clump    chomp**

It likes to _____ on plants, bugs, and eggs, too.

**6. chat    sandwich**

I eat an egg _____ for a snack!

**7. ostrich    odd**

An _____ eats plants, sand, and bugs.

**8. switch    chicken**

One of its eggs is like 24 _____ eggs. That is very big!

**9. quench    champ**

It runs very fast, too. The ostrich is such a _____!

Name _____  Date _____

# High Frequency Words

Trace each High Frequency Word and then write it.

wait wait

know know

other other

warm warm

year year

yellow yellow

world world

without without

# Word Cards: Words with *ch, tch*

| | | | |
|---|---|---|---|
| chest | watch | champ | patch |
| itch | children | chimp | pitch |
| lunchbox | chatting | batch | check |
| chill | catch | fetch | stretch |
| chin | switch | attach | chick |
| scratch | kitchen | stitch | hatch |
| rich | bench | ditch | inch |

# High Frequency Word Cards

| | |
|---|---|
| with | other |
| their | know |
| be | year |
| them | without |
| your | wait |
| down | warm |
| they | world |
| or | yellow |

For use with TE p. T99i

Unit 2 | Staying Alive

# Words with *th, wh*

Circle the word that names the picture.

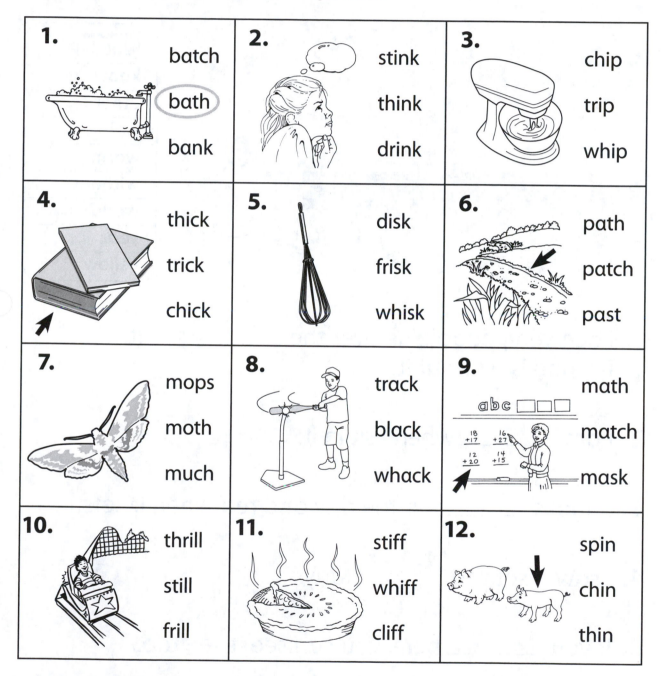

**1.**
batch
(bath)
bank

**2.**
stink
think
drink

**3.**
chip
trip
whip

**4.**
thick
trick
chick

**5.**
disk
frisk
whisk

**6.**
path
patch
past

**7.**
mops
moth
much

**8.**
track
black
whack

**9.**
math
match
mask

**10.**
thrill
still
frill

**11.**
stiff
whiff
cliff

**12.**
spin
chin
thin

**Read It Together**  What do you think? Is a moth thick or thin?

**High Frequency Words**

# What Is It?

Write a word from the box to complete each sentence.

| High Frequency Words |
| --- |
| know |
| other |
| wait |
| warm |
| without |
| world |
| year |
| yellow |

**1.** Each year, people all over the _____ see it.
No one is without it.

**2.** I am _____ when I sit in it.

**3.** It looks _____ in the day and red when it sets.

**4.** I saw it set the _____ day.

**5.** If you _____ here, you can see it set, too.

**6.** Do you _____ what it is? It is the sun!

Name _____ Date _____

# Sentences: Has, Have, Had

Cut cards. Spread both the gray cards and the white cards face up.
Choose one of each and say a sentence using those two words.

| has | have | had |
|-----|------|-----|
| I | you | he | she |
| it | we | they | cat |
| dog | horse | bird | fish |
| wings | tail | fur | feathers |
| scales | animals | pets | lions |
| teeth | friends | neighbors | parents |

**Phonics**

# Words with *th, wh*

Write the word that completes each sentence.

**1. sixth    whiff**

What is that smell? Did you get a _____ of it?

**2. think    wink**

I _____ Dad is in the kitchen!

**3. bring    broth**

That smell must be his chicken _____.

**4. thing    string**

It is the best _____ to eat for lunch.

**5. thick    chick**

It is not _____. It is thin.

**6. then    when**

I eat it _____ it is still warm!

**7. which    stitch**

There are buns and muffins, too. Dad asks _____ I want.

**8. wink    with**

I will have a bun _____ my broth.

**9. thank    whisk**

Then I _____ Dad for a very good lunch!

**Phonics**

# Contractions

| she + is = she's |
| can + not = can't |

**Write the contraction for the two underlined words on the line.**

**1.** You can see that <u>he</u> <u>is</u> sick.

You can see that _____ sick.

**2.** You can see that <u>she</u> <u>is</u> not sick.

You can see that _____ not sick.

**3.** Do you think <u>it</u> <u>is</u> fun to be sick?

Do you think _____ fun to be sick?

**4.** You <u>can</u> <u>not</u> be with your pals.

You _____ be with your pals.

**5.** You <u>do</u> <u>not</u> have much fun.

You _____ have much fun.

**Phonics**

# Contractions

| I + am = I'm |
|---|
| you + are = you're |

**Write the contraction for the two underlined words on the line.**

**1.** <u>I</u> <u>am</u> in the pond.

_____ in the pond.

**2.** <u>You</u> <u>are</u> in the pond, too.

_____ in the pond, too.

**3.** <u>We</u> <u>are</u> all wet!

_____ all wet!

**4.** My dog <u>can</u> <u>not</u> swim.

My dog _____ swim.

**5.** We <u>do</u> <u>not</u> let my dog jump into the pond!

We _____ let my dog jump into the pond!

Grammar and Writing

# Write Irregular Verbs

**Read the letter. Then choose a word from the box that goes with each sentence.**

| were | have | had |
|------|------|-----|
| has | was | is |

Dear Brandon,

I am having a great time at sea camp. This

camp ___has___ lots of cool things to do.

The water in the ocean _____ warm and

clear. That means it is easy to see fish. Yesterday, I

_____ fun on a boat. It _____ exciting to zoom

through the waves. Seagulls and other birds _____

all around the boat. I will come home Saturday. I

_____ a special surprise from sea camp for you!

Your friend,

Ali

# Living Lights

**Make a chart to compare bioluminescent animals.**

| How It Uses Light | Animal |
|---|---|
| to attract prey | glowworm<br><br>anglerfish |
| to send messages | |
| to hide | |
| | |

**Use your comparison chart to tell a partner about the animals in "Living Lights."**

**Phonics**

# Words with *sh, ph*

Circle the word that names the picture.

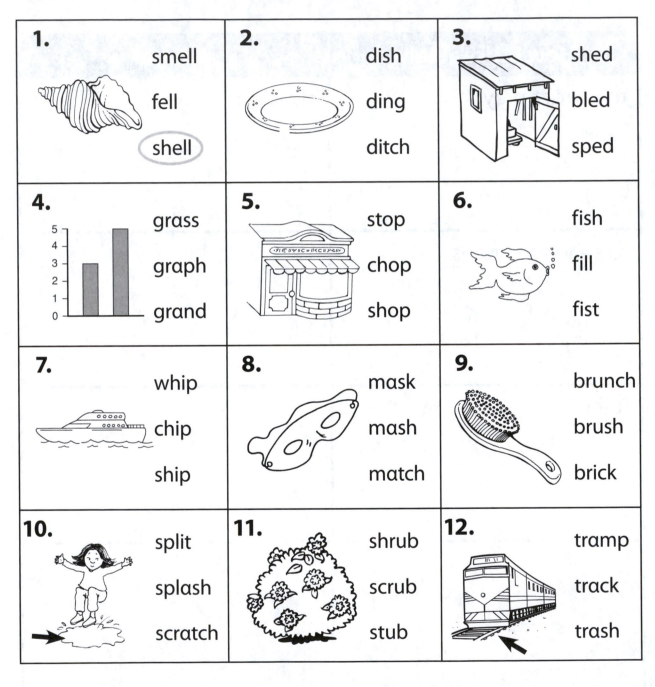

1.
smell
fell
shell

2.
dish
ding
ditch

3.
shed
bled
sped

4.
grass
graph
grand

5.
stop
chop
shop

6.
fish
fill
fist

7.
whip
chip
ship

8.
mask
mash
match

9.
brunch
brush
brick

10.
split
splash
scratch

11.
shrub
scrub
stub

12.
tramp
track
trash

**Read It Together**   She sells fish and shells at her shop.

Name _____ Date _____

# Words with *sh, ph*

Write the word that completes each sentence.

**1. graph    shellfish**

We can see _____ in this tank.

**2. shells    fresh**

They have no fins. They have _____.

**3. shrimp    squish**

This tank has _____ in it.

**4. swish    dolphins**

Over here are the _____.

**5. shock    fish**

They swim, but they are not _____.

**6. mammals    shrunk**

They are _____ like you and me!

**7. shack    splash**

Look out! They will _____ and get you wet!

**8. dash    damp**

Now we _____ over to see the man in the tank.

**9. shelf    wish**

I _____ I could swim in the tank with him!

**Handwriting**

# High Frequency Words

**Trace each High Frequency Word and then write it.**

call call

more more

than than

two two

walk walk

why why

young young

because because

# Word Cards: Words with *sh, ph*

| | | | |
|---|---|---|---|
| fish | shell | dolphin | phlox |
| wish | graph | splash | phone |
| bush | phase | push | phrase |
| dash | phonics | wash | orphan |
| shift | elephant | she | trophy |
| shelf | shut | alphabet | shrug |
| Phil | ashen | photo | shop |

For use with TE p. T121g      **PM2.43**      Unit 2 | Staying Alive

# High Frequency Word Cards

| | |
|---|---|
| other | call |
| know | more |
| year | two |
| without | walk |
| wait | than |
| warm | young |
| world | why |
| yellow | because |

For use with TE p. T121g  **PM2.44**  **Unit 2** | Staying Alive

Name _____ Date _____

# Compare Genres

Use a comparison chart to compare "Living Lights" and "Clever Creatures."

| Features | "Living Lights" | "Clever Creatures" |
|---|---|---|
| is about animals | ✓ | ✓ |
| includes words that rhyme | | ✓ |
| has facts | | |
| has photographs | | |
| has illustrations | | |
| | | |

Work with a partner. Read each feature and see if it is in "Living Lights" and "Clever Creatures." Make a check if you see the feature.

**PM2.45**

# Words with *-ed, -ing*

**Find the match for your card. Act it out.**

| | |
|---|---|
| **jump** | **kick** |
| **blink** | **stretch** |
| **jumped** | **jumping** |
| **kicked** | **kicking** |
| **blinked** | **blinking** |
| **stretched** | **stretching** |

**High Frequency Words**

# Walking the Dog

**Write a word from the box to complete each sentence.**

| High Frequency **Words** |
|---|
| because |
| call |
| more |
| than |
| two |
| walk |
| why |
| young |

**1.** I have a _____ dog. My dog is still a pup.

**2.** I _____ with my pup each day.

**3.** On some days, we go on _____ than one walk.

**4.** We go on _____ walks.

**5.** I call my pup to me now. _____ do I call her?

**6.** I call her _____ we are going on a walk!

**Grammar: Contractions**

# Use Contractions of *Be* and *Have*

**Directions:**

1. Take turns with a partner.

2. Toss a marker onto the game board.

3. Follow the directions in the square your marker lands on.

4. After you say your sentence, your partner follows these steps:

   • Say your partner's sentence with a contraction.

   • Say your partner's sentence with a contraction and *not*.

   • If your partner's sentence is singular, make it plural. If your partner's sentence is plural, make it singular.

| | |
|---|---|
| Say a sentence with <u>am</u>. | Say a sentence with <u>is</u>. |
| Say a sentence with <u>are</u>. | Say a sentence with <u>has</u>. |
| Say a sentence with <u>have</u>. | Say a sentence with <u>had</u>. |

# Words with *-ed, -ing*

**Write the word with *-ed* or *-ing* to complete each sentence.**

**1. go**

Gramps and Ben are _____ fishing.

**2. want**

Last year, Ben _____ to go, but he was too young.

**3. pack**

Ben just _____ all his fishing stuff.

**4. help**

Gramps _____ him.

**5. stand**

Now Gramps and Ben are _____ on the dock.

**6. splash**

The fish are _____ .

**7. pass**

One big fish just _____ by them!

**8. hand**

Ben is _____ Gramps his fishing rod.

**9. look**

He is _____ at the fish. That is more fun than catching them!

**Phonics**

# Plurals -s, -es

**Write the word with -ed or -ing to complete each sentence.**

**1. thing**

What _____ will we see if we walk down this path?

**2. fox**

Look over there! I see two _____ in the grass.

**3. branch**

What is up in those _____?

**4. nest**

I see two _____.

**5. egg**

There are little _____ in them.

**6. shrub**

Do you see those _____ by the pond?

**7. skunk**

Some _____ are under them.

**8. bench**

We can sit on the _____ over there.

**9. sandwich**

Then we can eat _____ for lunch.

**Grammar and Writing**

# Write Full Forms of *Be* and *Have*

**Read the report. Then choose words from the box that go with each sentence.**

| | | |
|---|---|---|
| has not | they are | she had |
| I am | I have | is not |

My name is Bella and ___I am___ interested in

animals, especially insects. I think _____ very

interesting. Did you know that not all bugs are

insects? Insects have six legs. A spider _____

an insect because it has eight legs. I love to read

books about insects. _____ just finished one

about insects that change color. I loaned it to my

sister Alex, but she _____ finished it yet. She said

_____ already started another book, so my bug

book would just have to wait!

# Insects at the Zoo

## Grammar Rules Verbs *be* and *have*

Verbs should match who or what they are telling about.

| For yourself, use | am | I **am** a scientist. |
|---|---|---|
| | have | I **have** work to do. |
| For one other person or thing, use | is | The Io moth **is** very clever. |
| | has | It **has** wings that look like big eyes. |
| For one other person, yourself and others, or other people and things, use | are | These wings **are** a clever trick. |
| | have | Many moths **have** features that keep them safe. |

**Choose the correct verb. Then read the sentence to a partner.**

1. My teacher ____*is*____ interested in all kinds of insects.
    is / are

2. He _____ good news for our class.
    has / have

3. We _____ on our way to the zoo on Friday!
    is / are

4. The zoo _____ a special place to see insects.
    has / have

5. I _____ excited about the trip to the zoo.
    am / is

6. You _____ invited to come, too!
    is / are

**Phonics**

# Words with Long *a*

Circle the word that goes with each picture.

**1.**
gap
gum
(game)

**2.**
rake
rack
rock

**3.**
cane
can
cap

**4.**
tape
tip
tap

**5.**
cap
cape
cup

**6.**
lack
lake
lock

**7.**
pluck
plate
pat

**8.**
whale
well
whack

**9.**
snack
snake
snap

**10.**
brag
brake
brick

**11.**
pan
plan
plane

**12.**
man
mane
mast

**Read It Together**    Do you see waves or rakes in the lake?

# Problem and Solution

Fill out a problem-and-solution chart.

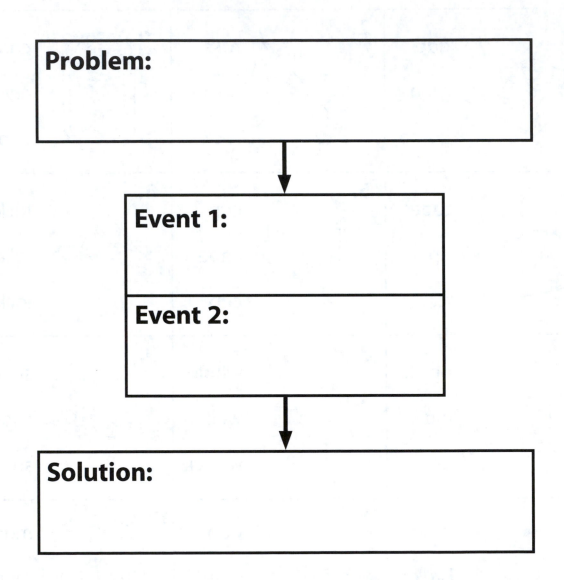

**Problem:**

**Event 1:**

**Event 2:**

**Solution:**

**Tell a partner about a problem you solved.**

# Adjectives and Nouns

Find an adjective and a noun that rhyme from the word banks.
Write the rhyming pair next to the riddle it answers.

| **Adjectives** | | |
|------|------|------|
| dry | wet | gray |
| dark | swell | loud |
| nice | damp | |

| **Nouns** | | |
|------|------|------|
| cloud | ice | sky |
| camp | park | pet |
| day | well | |

1. What is a soaked puppy called?     a ___*wet pet*___

2. What is smooth, frozen water called?     _____

3. What is a big tent after a rainfall called?     a _____

4. What is a rainy Monday called?     a _____

5. What is a playground during a strong
   storm called?     a _____

6. What is a lack of clouds called?     a _____

7. What is rumbling thunder called?     a _____

8. What is a great place to get
   water called?     a _____

For use with TE p. T133m     **PM3.3**     Unit 3 | Water for Everyone

**Phonics**

# Words with Long *a*

**Write the word that completes each sentence.**

**1. wade   cake**

Zane and Jake _____ into the lake.

**2. tack   take**

They _____ a quick dip and swim to the raft.

**3. tapes   waves**

Then Mom _____ at them, and they swim back.

**4. cave   make**

Zane finds a _____ in some rocks.

**5. bats   bakes**

What is in it? Are there _____ and snakes?

**6. manes   chases**

Jake _____ Zane back to Mom and Dad.

**7. snack   snake**

They _____ on sandwiches.

**8. states   grapes**

Then they eat a bunch of _____ .

**9. trade   late**

It gets _____ . They pack up and go back to their van.

Name _____  Date _____

# High Frequency Words

Trace each High Frequency Word and then write it.

cold cold

form form

turn turn

drink drink

live live

water water

feel feel

three three

For use with TE p. T138f          **PM3.5**          Unit 3 | Water for Everyone

# Word Cards: Long *a*

| | | | |
|---|---|---|---|
| lake | game | tape | plate |
| date | shake | flake | came |
| shape | drape | state | snake |
| flame | wake | name | gate |
| late | same | take | frame |
| cape | crate | scrape | brake |
| skate | quake | blame | grape |

For use with TE p. T133k  **PM3.6**  **Unit 3** | Water for Everyone

# High Frequency Word Cards

| | |
|---|---|
| back | cold |
| how | drink |
| those | feel |
| body | form |
| into | live |
| way | three |
| eat | turn |
| these | water |

Name _____ Date _____

# Syllables

Circle the word that goes with each picture.

| | | |
|---|---|---|
| **1.** channel / chase / champs | **2.** panes / pancakes / pandas | **3.** scallop / scab / skate |
| **4.** cascade / cape / cupcake | **5.** frame / frank / frantic | **6.** vase / invade / vane |
| **7.** upstate / unmade / upset | **8.** exam / exit / exhale | **9.** snack / snake / snap |
| **10.** unsafe / unlace / subtract | **11.** end / escape / engrave | **12.** 2 + 2 3 / make / mistrust / mistake |

**Read It Together**   Do you like cupcakes or pancakes?

For use with TE p. T141c          **PM3.8**          Unit 3 | Water for Everyone

**High Frequency Words**

# At the Lake

**Write a word from the box to complete each sentence.**

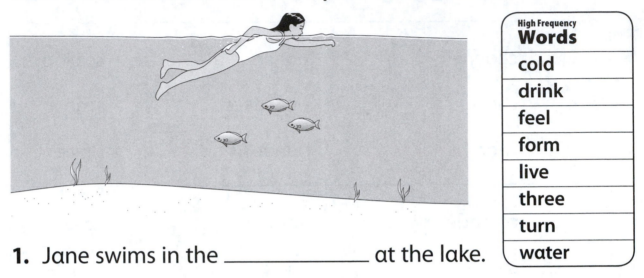

| High Frequency Words |
|---|
| cold |
| drink |
| feel |
| form |
| live |
| three |
| turn |
| water |

1. Jane swims in the _____ at the lake.

2. It feels very _____ .

3. Fish live in the lake. Jane sees _____ swim by.

4. Then they _____ back and swim by Jane.

5. Jane gets out of the lake and has a _____ of water.

6. This _____ of water is good to drink!

**Phonics**

# Syllables

Divide each word into syllables. Then write the word that completes each sentence.

**1. invade    nickname**

I am Jackson, but my _____ is Jack.

**2. shameful    escape**

Mom smiles and says the things I do are _____ .

**3. unmade    exhale**

She does not like it when my bed is _____ !

**4. translate    mistake**

I made a big _____ when I let the dog escape!

**5. inhales    pancakes**

Then there was the big mess when I made _____ !

**6. unsafe    inflate**

I spilled milk, and she said the mess was _____ .

**7. cupcakes    inflates**

But Mom has a big hug and _____ for me. Yum!

Name _____ Date _____

# Write Adjectives

| Adjectives That Describe | | Adjectives That Compare | | Adjectives That Signal | |
|---|---|---|---|---|---|
| fresh | a lot | faster | fastest | this | that |
| huge | bright | bigger | biggest | these | those |
| yellow | three | softer | softest | | |

**Read the adjectives on the chart. Choose adjectives to complete the sentences.**

1. Rain did not fall for _____*three*_____ weeks.

2. The sun was _____ and hot.

3. We want to catch rain in pails by _____ porch.

4. The round pail is _____ than the square pail.

5. A _____ cloud forms in the dark sky.

6. Rain! _____ water from that cloud fills our pails.

# Vocabulary Bingo

1. Write one Key Word in each cloud.

2. Listen to the clues. Find the Key Word and use a marker to cover it.

3. Say "Bingo" when you have four markers in a row.

Name ______________________ Date ____________

Problem-and-Solution Chart

# Frog Brings Rain

**Use a problem-and-solution chart to tell about "Frog Brings Rain."**

**Problem:** First Woman needs Water to put out Fire.

↓

**Event 1:** She asks Hunting People to take Water to Fire.

↓

**Event 2:**

↓

**Solution:**

**Use your chart to tell a partner how First Woman and Frog solve the problem.**

**Phonics**

# Words with Long *i*

Circle the word that names the picture.

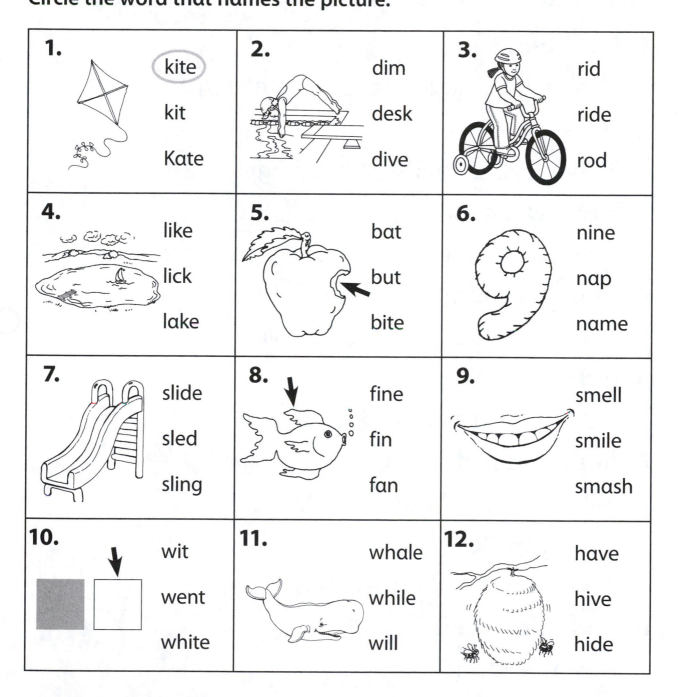

1.
kite
kit
Kate

2.
dim
desk
dive

3.
rid
ride
rod

4.
like
lick
lake

5.
bat
but
bite

6.
nine
nap
name

7.
slide
sled
sling

8.
fine
fin
fan

9.
smell
smile
smash

10.
wit
went
white

11.
whale
while
will

12.
have
hive
hide

**Read It Together**   Do you like to use a kite, a bike, or a slide?

**Phonics**

# Words with Long *i*

Write the word that completes each sentence.

**1. life   beside**

Mike and his dad sit _____ their tent.

**2. dine   wide**

They _____ on fish, rice, and grapes.

**3. size   while**

Mike sees a snake _____ they eat.

**4. bite   sunshine**

The snake does not _____ Mike.

**5. hides   miles**

It _____ in some rocks.

**6. lines   describes**

Mike _____ the snake to his dad.

**7. rise   reptile**

Dad tells Mike that a snake is a _____.

**8. bedtime   prize**

Now it is late. It is _____.

**9. five   inside**

Mike and Dad rest _____ their tent.

Name _____ Date _____

# High Frequency Words

**Trace each High Frequency Word and then write it.**

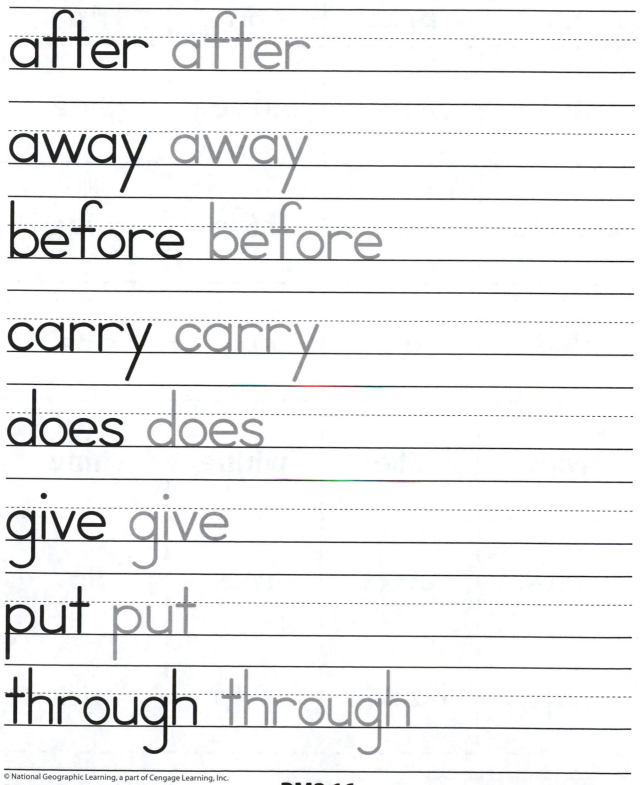

after after

away away

before before

carry carry

does does

give give

put put

through through

# Word Cards: Long *i*, Short *i*

| | | | |
|---|---|---|---|
| pine | prize | hit | rip |
| strike | insist | outside | glide |
| combine | sit | hide | pride |
| hid | dip | quip | side |
| wipe | like | whine | shine |
| pick | strict | trick | lip |
| mitten | napkin | drip | brick |

For use with TE p. T159g          **PM3.17**          **Unit 3** | Water for Everyone

# High Frequency Word Cards

| | |
|---|---|
| now | put |
| over | give |
| under | does |
| very | away |
| could | before |
| good | after |
| part | through |
| hard | carry |

For use with TE p. T159g      **PM3.18**      Unit 3 | Water for Everyone

Name _____  Date _____

# Compare Explanations

Show how the two explanations for rain are different.

| How Is Rain Made? | |
|---|---|
| **Traditional Tale Explanation** | **Science Experiment Explanation** |
| • Frog carries water. | • Warm, wet air rises. |

**Ask a partner questions about the story and the science experiment.**

For use with TE p. T163g          **PM3.19**          **Unit 3** | Water for Everyone

Name _____  Date _____

# Words with Long *o*

Circle the word that names the picture.

| 1. 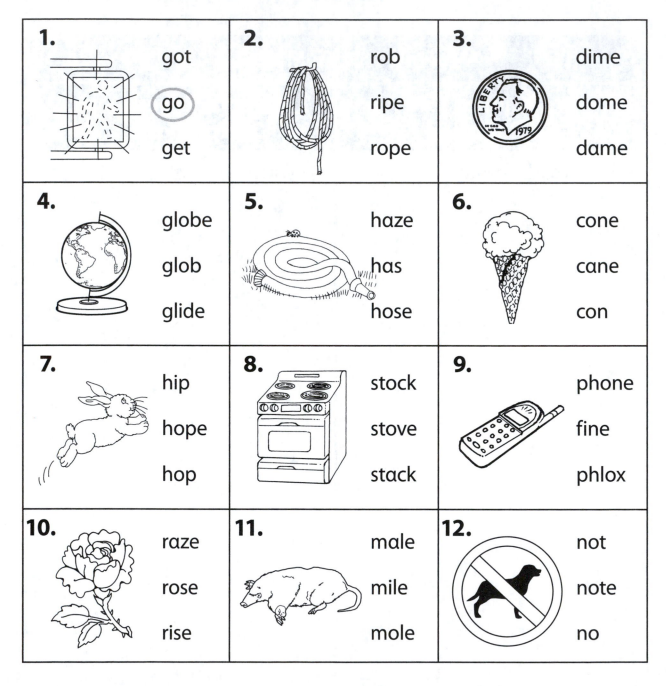 | 2. | 3. |
|---|---|---|
| got / (go) / get | rob / ripe / rope | dime / dome / dame |
| **4.** globe / glob / glide | **5.** haze / has / hose | **6.** cone / cane / con |
| **7.** hip / hope / hop | **8.** stock / stove / stack | **9.** phone / fine / phlox |
| **10.** raze / rose / rise | **11.** male / mile / mole | **12.** not / note / no |

**Read It Together**   Do you water with a hose, a rose, or a stove?

# In the Bag

**Write a word from the box to complete each sentence.**

| High Frequency **Words** |
|---|
| after |
| away |
| before |
| carry |
| does |
| give |
| put |
| through |

**1.** Mom and Dad _____ a bag.

**2.** They _____ it down and step away from it. What's inside the bag?

**3.** "_____ us some hints," we beg.

**4.** So, _____ we look, Dad does.

**5.** "It does not have legs, and it swims _____ water," Dad says.

**6.** _____ we get those hints, we know it is a fish!

Name _____  Date _____

# Mix and Match Sentences

Choose one item from each column. Say a sentence using all three parts. Then ask your partner to say the same sentence, changing one part.

| A | B | C |
|---|---|---|
| a<br>an<br>the | hour<br>river<br>rain<br>cloud<br>well<br>hole<br>honest | ruined my plans<br>is very deep<br>that Dad dug<br>is moving swiftly<br>covers the sun<br>passed by slowly<br>person I know<br>your new shoes<br>runs by the town<br>will stop soon<br>has a cover on it<br>is a long time<br>hides the moon<br>is big and dark<br>holds lots of fish<br>is good for our garden<br>has a bucket on a rope<br>wait by the park |

**Phonics**

# Words with Long *o*

Write the word that completes each sentence.

**1. throne    go**

I _____ on a hike at camp.

**2. tadpoles    closes**

We see some _____ in the pond.

**3. so    froze**

They look _____ much like little fish.

**4. quote    suppose**

I _____ they will be frogs one day!

**5. holes    explodes**

Look over there! Do you see the _____ by those stones?

**6. moles    trombones**

Do you think they were made by _____ or snakes?

**7. opposes    pinecones**

We see twigs and _____ that came down in the wind.

**8. broke    flagpole**

Now it is time to go and sit beside the _____.

**9. rotate    home**

Then it will be time to get on the bus to go _____.

**Grammar and Writing**

# Write Adjectives and Articles

Read the story. Then write a word from the box to complete each sentence.

| dry | hungry | wet | a | an | the | those |
|-----|--------|-----|---|----|----|-------|

Brodie and his family decided to go for _____*a*_____ hike.

The hike would take several hours. Brodie took _____

apple and a granola bar in his backpack. Hiking always

made him _____.

After hiking for a while, Brodie's mom looked up at

_____ sky. "Uh-oh," she said. "Look at _____ dark

clouds. We might get _____." "No way!" answered

Brodie. "My poncho will keep me _____."

**Grammar and Writing**
# After the Storm

> ## Grammar Rules  Adjectives and Articles
>
> | | |
> |---|---|
> | An **adjective** can describe what a noun is like. | → A **light** rain starts to fall.<br>The raindrops feel **icy** and **cold**. |
> | An **article** can tell which noun you mean. | → <u>**A**</u> cloud fills up with water.<br>Raindrops fall on <u>**the**</u> green hill.<br>It is <u>**an**</u> amazing thing to see. |

**Add adjectives and articles.**

The storm lasted for ___*three*___ days. Then the _____

sun rose. It dried up the _____ grass. _____ puddles

started to disappear. Then we looked up into the _____

sky. There was _____ amazing rainbow. It looked

_____ and _____. Soon the weather was _____

and _____ again.

**Tell a partner about weather you like. Use adjectives and articles.**

**Phonics**

# Words with Long e

Write the letters to name each picture.

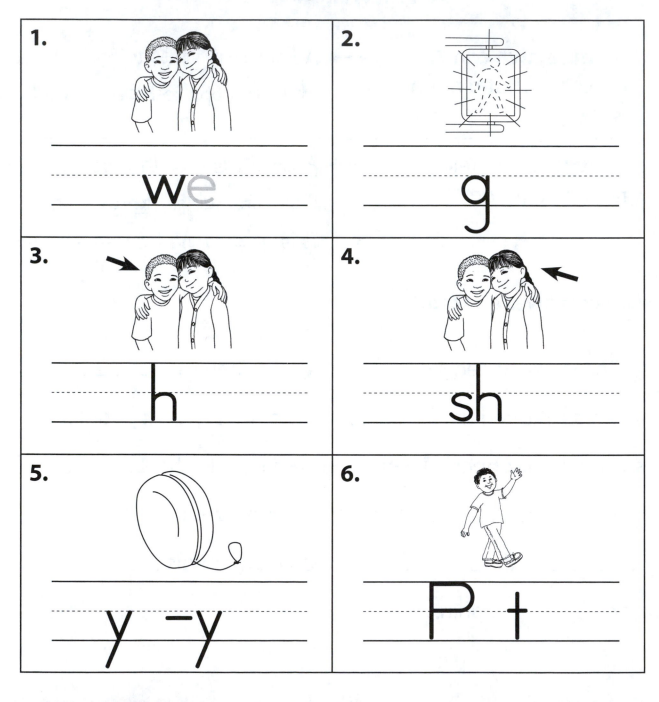

1. we

2. g

3. h

4. sh

5. y -y

6. P t

**Read It Together**   We go to get Pete's yo-yo.

# Cause and Effect

Fill out a cause-and-effect chart to show what happened when you did something.

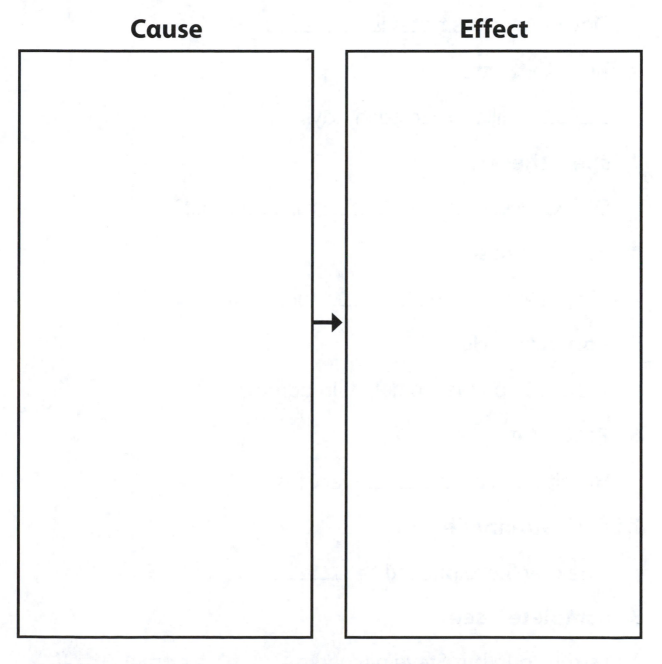

**Cause**                    **Effect**

💬 Tell a partner about what happened and why.

**Phonics**

# Words with Long e

**Write the word that completes each sentence.**

**1. theme   Eve**

One of my classmates is _____.

**2. We   Extreme**

_____ like to run each day.

**3. she   these**

Did you know that _____ runs very fast?

**4. egg   athlete**

My pal Steve is an _____, too.

**5. Concrete   He**

_____ pitches to help win games.

**6. Pete   be**

His pitches can _____ very fast.

**7. me   stampede**

One day Steve pitched to _____.

**8. complete   see**

I struck out, but Steve pitched a _____ game!

**Phonics**

# Syllables

Write short vowel words from the box under *pen* and long vowel words under *so*.

| he | not | no | be | cap | sun |
|------|------|------|------|------|------|
| web | him | hi | leg | she | go |

| **pen** | **so** |
|---------|--------|
| 1. _____ | 7. _____ |
| 2. _____ | 8. _____ |
| 3. _____ | 9. _____ |
| 4. _____ | 10. _____ |
| 5. _____ | 11. _____ |
| 6. _____ | 12. _____ |

Name _____ Date _____

# High Frequency Words

Trace each High Frequency Word and then write it.

our our _____

stop stop _____

take take _____

off off _____

clean clean _____

let let _____

think think _____

going going _____

# Word Cards: Long *e*, Short *e*

| | | | |
|---|---|---|---|
| me | we | bed | pencil |
| these | tennis | she | met |
| bell | Pete | get | here |
| complete | well | stampede | relax |
| web | felt | before | wet |
| decide | he | swell | begin |
| cobweb | theme | fell | men |

# High Frequency Word Cards

| | |
|---|---|
| other | off |
| know | going |
| year | clean |
| without | stop |
| wait | think |
| warm | our |
| world | let |
| yellow | take |

# Endings -s, -ed, -ing

Cut out the cards and mix them up. Match the cards and tell how the ending changes the word.

| | |
|:---:|:---:|
| wave | waves |
| waved | waving |
| hop | hops |
| hopped | hopping |
| smile | smiles |
| smiled | smiling |

High Frequency Words

# Mop It Up!

**Write a word from the box to complete each sentence.**

| High Frequency **Words** |
| --- |
| clean |
| going |
| let |
| off |
| our |
| stop |
| take |
| think |

**1.** It is time to _____ our home.

**2.** I am _____ to help mop.

**3.** I _____ that is a fun job to do.

**4.** Mom and Dad _____ me fill the bucket with water.

**5.** Suds pop up. I turn the water off, but I can't _____ the suds! They go all over!

**6.** I have to _____ my mop and wipe up the suds!

Name _____  Date _____

# Say Sentences

**Directions:**

1. Make a spinner.

2. Play with a partner.

3. Take turns spinning the spinner.

4. Say a sentence using the adverb on the spinner.

5. Then your partner says a sentence using the same adverb.

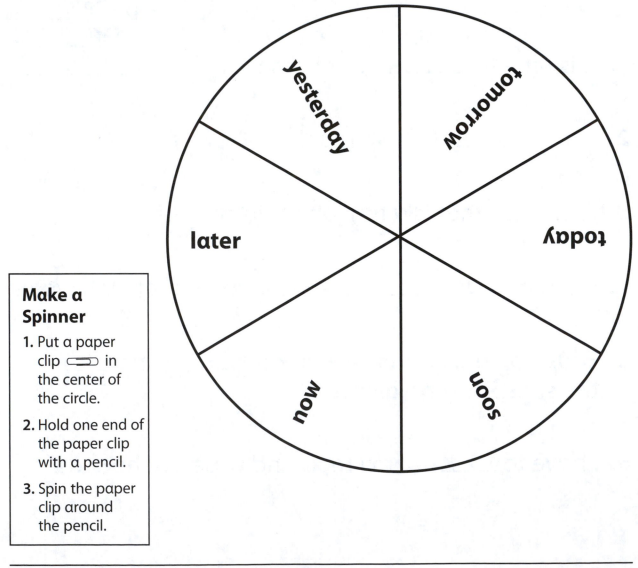

**Make a Spinner**

1. Put a paper clip in the center of the circle.

2. Hold one end of the paper clip with a pencil.

3. Spin the paper clip around the pencil.

**Phonics**

# Endings -s, -ed, -<u>ing</u>

| | |
|---|---|
| grin  + s        = grins | bake + s          = bakes |
| grin  + n + ed = grinned | grin  + n + ing = grinning |
| bake - e + ed = baked | bake – e + ing = baking |

**Write the word with the correct ending to complete each sentence.**

**1. run**

Tam is _____ on the path.

**2. wave**

She just passed her pal Ben and _____ to him.

**3. stop**

Ben was skating but had _____ to rest.

**4. smile**

When Tam ran by, Ben _____ at her.

**5. chase**

Now Ben hops up and is _____ Tam. Will he catch her?

**6. get**

The two pals are _____ close to the end of the path.

**7. hope**

Tam runs fast and _____ that she will win!

**Grammar and Writing**

# Write Adverbs

**Read the letter. Then choose a word from the box that goes with each sentence.**

| soon | swiftly | yesterday | quickly | slowly |
|------|---------|-----------|---------|--------|

Dear Megan,

   Our rafting trip was awesome! I had so much fun _yesterday_.

The river ran _____, but we still tried to paddle. We

sometimes got splashed, but we dried out _____ in the

sun. Now I have to walk _____ because all my muscles

hurt. I hope I can go rafting again really _____, though.

                    Your friend,

                    Kate

**Cause-and-Effect Chart**

# Cause and Effect

Fill out a cause-and-effect chart to show the results of things that happened in "PlayPumps."

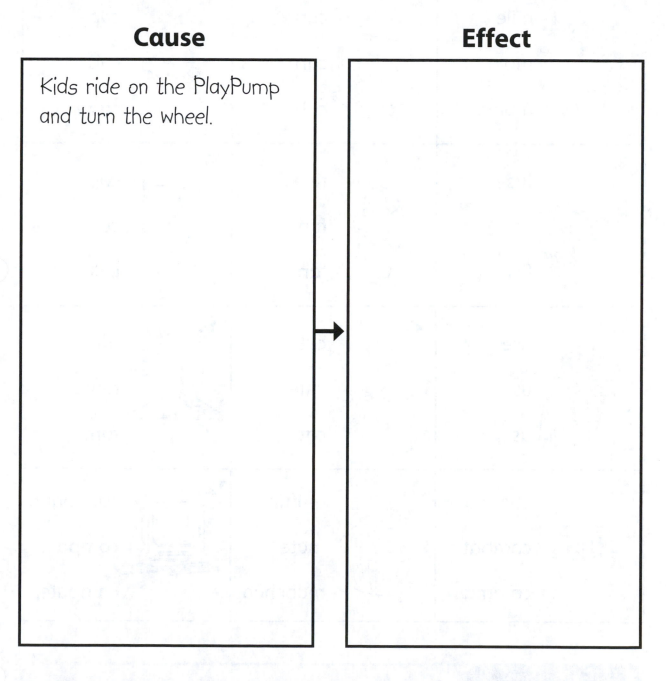

## Cause

Kids ride on the PlayPump and turn the wheel.

## Effect

💬 **Use your chart to tell a partner about more causes and effects in "PlayPumps."**

Name _____     Date _____

# Words with *u_e*

Circle the word that names the picture.

1.
mile
mole
(mule)

2.
cube
cub
cab

3.
cap
cup
cape

4.
fuse
fuss
fist

5.
fine
fun
fan

6.
cap
cute
cut

7.
use
us
as

8.
cut
cute
cat

9.
fun
fame
fume

10.
commute
combat
comma

11.
muffin
mute
munched

12.
command
compact
computer

**Read It Together**   Do you think that a mule is cute?

**Phonics**

# Words with *u_e*

Write the word that completes each sentence.

**1. commutes   cubes**

Dave _____ to his job each day.

**2. dispute   mule**

He doesn't ride a _____ to his job in the city.

**3. fuse   bus**

He rides a _____.

**4. fumes   ducklings**

On some days, there are a lot of _____ from the bus.

**5. Excuse   Truck**

One day a man stopped Dave and said, "_____ me."

**6. confused   tugged**

The man was _____ because he was lost.

**7. hundred   used**

Dave _____ a map to help the man find his way.

**8. shrug   cute**

Dave has a _____ little dog.

**9. pup   accuse**

When Dave is at his job, I take his _____ for walks.

Name _____ Date _____

# High Frequency Words

Trace each High Frequency Word and then write it.

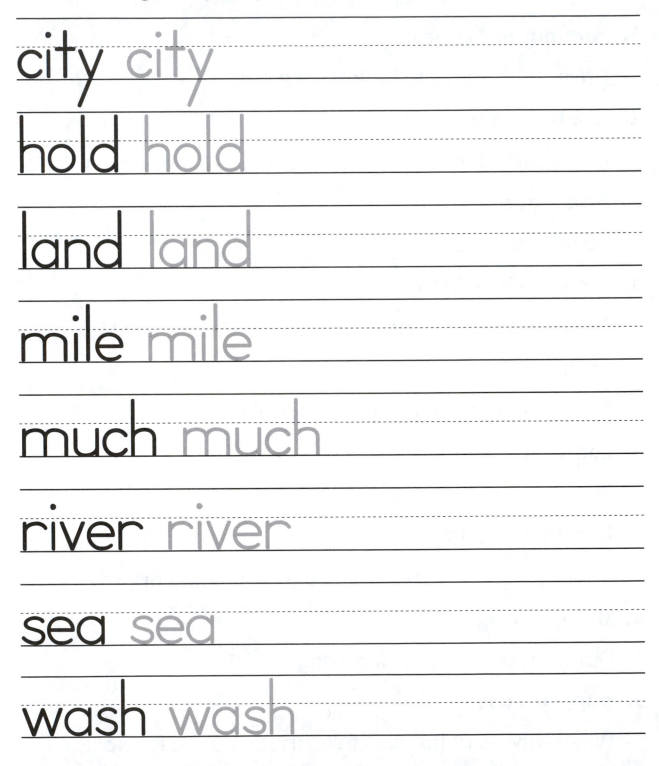

city city

hold hold

land land

mile mile

much much

river river

sea sea

wash wash

For use with TE p. T191c          **PM3.41**          **Unit 3** | Water for Everyone

# Word Cards: *u_e*

| cube | mule | flute | drum |
| hut | sun | use | fuse |
| cute | fume | mutt | tub |
| put | club | compute | excuse |
| stuck | include | tube | rude |
| June | glum | cut | prune |
| hug | spruce | bun | fun |

# High Frequency Word Cards

| | |
|---|---|
| call | land |
| more | wash |
| two | city |
| walk | much |
| than | river |
| young | hold |
| why | sea |
| because | mile |

Name _____  Date _____

# Compare Information

Use a comparison chart to compare "PlayPumps" and "The Mighty Colorado."

| How People Get Water | |
|---|---|
| **"PlayPumps"** | **"The Mighty Colorado"** |
| • Kids play. | |

💬 **Share your chart with a partner. Take turns asking questions about the information.**

Name _____ Date _____

# More Words with *u_e*

Circle the word that names the picture.

1.
flake
(flute)
flunk

2.
rod
rude
ride

3.
tube
tub
tab

4.
prune
prone
print

5.
tent
tune
tine

6.
crust
crude
crab

7.
plant
plum
plume

8.
June
jam
just

9.
dens
dines
dunes

10.
like
Luke
lake

11.
rocket
rule
role

12.
confuse
complete
costume

**Read It Together**     One rule is not to be rude.

**High Frequency Words**

# Home by the Sea

**Write words from the box to complete each sentence.**

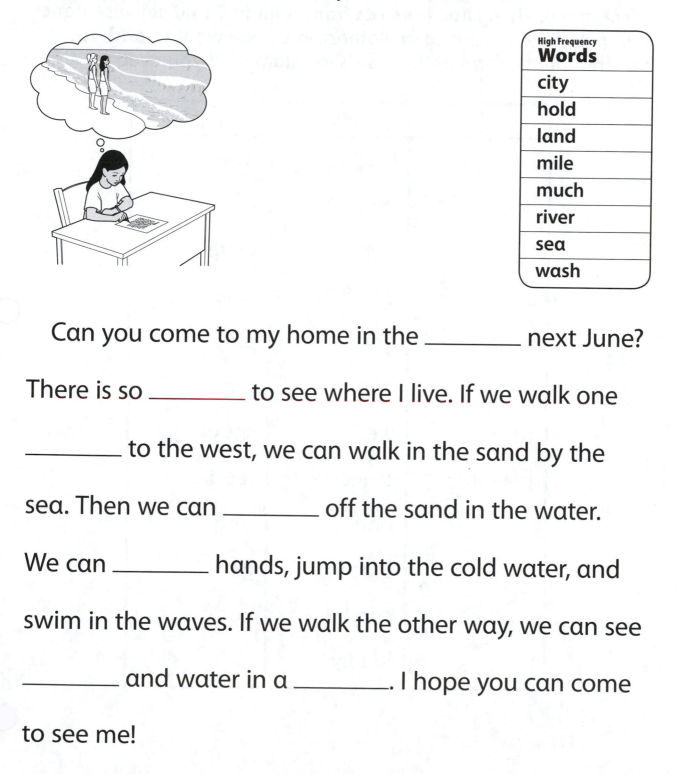

| High Frequency Words |
|---|
| city |
| hold |
| land |
| mile |
| much |
| river |
| sea |
| wash |

Can you come to my home in the _____ next June?

There is so _____ to see where I live. If we walk one

_____ to the west, we can walk in the sand by the

sea. Then we can _____ off the sand in the water.

We can _____ hands, jump into the cold water, and

swim in the waves. If we walk the other way, we can see

_____ and water in a _____. I hope you can come

to see me!

Grammar: Adjectives and Articles

# Mix and Match Sentences

First choose a word from column A. Then choose one of the words in column B. Then choose words from column C and say a sentence using all three parts and any other words you want to add. You can change the form of the words in column C if you need to.

| A | B | C |
|---|---|---|
| I | loud | walk |
| you | badly | yell |
| he | quick | write |
| she | carefully | stop |
| it | good | play |
| we | quietly | run |
| they | well | shout |
| person | quiet | read |
| | bad | sing |
| | quickly | go |
| | careful | eat |
| | loudly | fix |

# More Words with *u_e*

Write the word that completes each sentence.

**1. flutes   dunes**

My class is going on a trip to the sand _____.

**2. includes   prunes**

The trip _____ time for hiking and time for lunch.

**3. intrudes   rules**

Mr. Chang gave us some _____ for the trip.

**4. tunes   costumes**

We may sing _____ on the bus, but we may not yell.

**5. rude   excuse**

We must not be _____ to each other and to people we see.

**6. pollute   plume**

We must not _____ while we are there, and we must take our trash back to the bus with us.

**7. assumes   tubes**

He _____ that we will be good!

**8. mules   concludes**

He _____ that if we are good, we will all have fun.

# Write Adverbs

**Read the letter. Then choose a word from the box that goes with each sentence.**

| here | there | somewhere | well | smoothly | swiftly |
|------|-------|-----------|------|----------|---------|

Max was riding on a little raft through the Grand Canyon. The river rushed _____*swiftly*_____ through the canyon. The family rafting trip was going _____. After some rough water, the raft was gliding _____ down the river. Max heard a loud sound _____ high over his head. He looked in the sky and saw a big hawk flying up _____. *I cannot believe I am* _____, *thought Max. I am as happy as that hawk must be.*

Grammar: Adverbs

# Adverb Tic-Tac-Toe

1. **Play with a partner.**

2. **Player 1 chooses and reads the sentence. Player 2 tells if the adverb tells how or when.**

3. **Player 2 marks the square if the answer is correct.**

4. **Then players switch roles.**

5. **Keep taking turns to see if one player can get three marks in a row.**

| | | |
|---|---|---|
| The water stopped <u>yesterday</u>. | We <u>quickly</u> called the plumber. | The plumber arrived <u>soon</u>. |
| The plumber worked <u>carefully</u> to find the clog. | She <u>finally</u> found the clog. | <u>Then</u> she cleared it up. |
| <u>Slowly</u> the water began to flow. | We have plenty of water <u>today</u>. | We <u>gladly</u> fill our water jugs. |

**Phonics**

# Words with *ai, ay*

**Circle the word that names the picture.**

**1.**
sell
(sail)
sill

**2.**
ray
rat
rail

**3.**
may
mill
mail

**4.**
ran
rain
rake

**5.**
hit
hail
hay

**6.**
jail
jay
jell

**7.**
chain
chin
children

**8.**
trap
trail
tray

**9.**
bray
braid
brad

**10.**
snack
say
snail

**11.**
paint
pant
pays

**12.**
sprain
spray
sprint

**Read It Together**   Jay paints trains on gray days when it rains.

**PM4.1**

Name _____  Date _____

# Character Traits

Make a character map. Write about two characters you know.

| Character | What the Character Does | What the Character Is Like |
|---|---|---|
|  |  |  |

💬 **Tell a partner which character was your favorite and why.**

# Words with *ai, ay*

Unscramble the word and use it in a sentence.

| | |
|---|---|
| **1. a h y** <br><br> __ __ __ __ <br><br> _____ <br><br> _____ | **2. n i r a** <br><br> __ __ __ __ __ <br><br> _____ <br><br> _____ |
| **3. i a l s** <br><br> __ __ __ __ __ <br><br> _____ <br><br> _____ | **4. y a w** <br><br> __ __ __ __ <br><br> _____ <br><br> _____ |
| **5. y c a l** <br><br> __ __ __ __ __ <br><br> _____ <br><br> _____ | **6. t i n a r** <br><br> __ __ __ __ __ __ <br><br> _____ <br><br> _____ |
| **7. t i w a** <br><br> __ __ __ __ __ <br><br> _____ <br><br> _____ | **8. s l y p a** <br><br> __ __ __ __ __ __ <br><br> _____ <br><br> _____ |

**Phonics**

# Syllables with *ai, ay*

Divide the syllables. Circle the word that names the picture.

| 1. | 2. | 3. |
|---|---|---|
| (raining) / resting | fainted / painted | playing / paying |
| **4.** | **5.** | **6.** |
| mailing / rushing | braided / waited | spraying / staying |
| **7.** | **8.** | **9.** |
| saying / sailing | paying / playing | staying / saying |

**Read It Together**   We like playing when it is raining.

**Handwriting**

# High Frequency Words

Trace each High Frequency Word and then write it.

don't don't

door door

about about

work work

should should

want want

where where

important important

# Word Cards: Words with *ai, ay*

| | | | |
|---|---|---|---|
| rain | train | hay | spray |
| aid | sprain | main | yesterday |
| stain | tray | day | hail |
| maintain | pail | play | fail |
| waiting | paid | pain | say |
| stay | regain | away | plain |
| delay | decay | pray | always |

# High Frequency Word Cards

| | |
|---|---|
| live | don't |
| feel | door |
| water | about |
| cold | work |
| drink | should |
| turn | want |
| three | where |
| form | important |

For use with TE p. T199k     **PM4.7**     **Unit 4** | Lend a Hand

**Phonics**

# Syllable Division

Divide the syllables. Circle the word that names the picture.

| 1. | ostrich <br> oven <br> (open) | 2. | zigzag <br> zebra <br> zapped | 3. | email <br> even <br> enter |
| --- | --- | --- | --- | --- | --- |
| 4. | melon <br> misses <br> moment | 5. | racket <br> rapid <br> radish | 6. | robot <br> rotate <br> ruler |
| 7. | satin <br> salad <br> setup | 8. | minus <br> music <br> menu | 9. | cabin <br> comet <br> cobra |
| 10. | second <br> seven <br> solid | 11. | robin <br> relax <br> remake | 12. | debate <br> dolphin <br> donut |

**Read It Together**   Is there a zebra or a radish in the salad?

Name _____ Date _____

# Who Brings the Mail?

Write a word from the box to complete each sentence.

| High Frequency Words |
| --- |
| about |
| don't |
| door |
| important |
| should |
| want |
| where |
| work |

**1.** People who bring mail have an _____ job to do.

**2.** They _____ hard, and we should thank them!

**3.** They _____ bring mail on Sundays.

**4.** My mailman puts mail in the box by my _____.

**5.** _____ does your mail go?

**6.** I want to find out more _____ this job because I want to be a mailman!

Grammar: Sentences

# Mix and Match Sentences

First choose a naming part from column A. Then choose a telling part from column B. Say a complete sentence using both parts and any other words you want to add.

| A | B |
|---|---|
| girl | tumble |
| people | save |
| eggs | snatch |
| lion | fly |
| mouse | yell |
| he | catch |
| they | go |
| farmer | help |
| animals | live |
| eagle | smash |
| wall | cry |
| rocks | chew |

**Phonics**

# Syllable Division

**Divide the syllables. Write the word that completes each sentence.**

**1. frozen    photo**

Can you find me in this _____?

**2. female    panic**

I am the _____ who is playing the trombone!

**3. minus    music**

I play all kinds of _____ on my trombone.

**4. even    exit**

I can _____ play some jazz.

**5. email    seven**

In fact, I will play _____ jazz songs for you!

**6. oval    second**

The _____ song is the one I like best.

**7. moment    bison**

Wait for one _____ .

**8. begin    panic**

Now I will _____ to play.

**9. comics    never**

I hope that I _____ stop playing my trombone!

**Grammar and Writing**

# Write Complete Sentences

**Read the story. Then choose the word or words from the word box that correctly complete each sentence. Write the words.**

| the little things | somebody |
|---|---|
| am going to the animal shelter | my sister and I |
| could not take care of themselves | we |

Today I _am going to the animal shelter_ . _____

both help clean the shelter and play with the dogs and

cats. _____ dropped off a box of kittens last

night. The tiny kittens _____ .

_____ mewed loudly and tried to climb out

of their box. _____ picked them up and fed

them from a bottle.

**Character Map**

# Aesop's Fables

Make a character map to tell about the characters in "Aesop's Fables."

| Character | What the Character Does | What the Character Is Like |
|---|---|---|
| the lion | lets the mouse leave | generous |
| Farmer Bean | | |
| | | |
| | | |

💬 **Use your character map to tell a partner about the characters in "Aesop's Fables."**

**Phonics**

# Words with ee

Circle the word that names the picture.

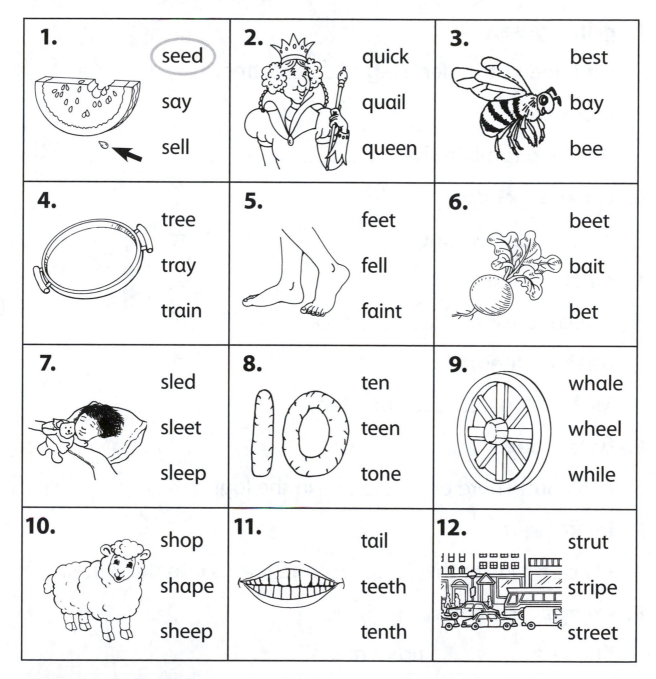

**1.**
- (seed)
- say
- sell

**2.**
- quick
- quail
- queen

**3.**
- best
- bay
- bee

**4.**
- tree
- tray
- train

**5.**
- feet
- fell
- faint

**6.**
- beet
- bait
- bet

**7.**
- sled
- sleet
- sleep

**8.**
- ten
- teen
- tone

**9.**
- whale
- wheel
- while

**10.**
- shop
- shape
- sheep

**11.**
- tail
- teeth
- tenth

**12.**
- strut
- stripe
- street

**Read It Together**   Sixteen sheep sleep by the street.

For use with TE p. T223m                    **PM4.14**                    **Unit 4** | Lend a Hand

**Phonics**

# Words with *ee*

**Write the word that completes each sentence.**

**1. grin   green**

Dad and I sit under a big _____ tree.

**2. trip   tree**

We see a robin in the _____.

**3. cheeps   chaps**

It _____ its song.

**4. twists   tweets**

A second robin _____ back.

**5. peeks   seems**

My big dog _____ at a log.

**6. bets   bees**

Look out! There are _____ in the log!

**7. leek   lake**

My dog runs to the _____ and jumps into the water.

**8. creeps   crayons**

Then he _____ up to me.

**9. slaps   sleeps**

He shakes himself off, plops down, and _____.

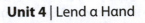

Name _____ Date _____

# Contractions

| I | + would | = I'd |
| she | + will | = she'll |
| they | + have | = they've |

**Write the contraction that completes each sentence.**

**1.** <u>I would</u> like a lemon muffin.

_____ like a lemon muffin.

**2.** Look! <u>They have</u> got three muffins on a plate.

Look! _____ got three muffins on a plate.

**3.** I think <u>she will</u> take one plain muffin.

I think _____ take one plain muffin.

**4.** I see that <u>you have</u> got one nut muffin.

I see that _____ got one nut muffin.

**5.** I know <u>there will</u> be one lemon muffin left for me!

I know _____ be one lemon muffin left for me!

**Handwriting**

# High Frequency Words

Trace each High Frequency Word and then write it.

house house

kind kind

place place

both both

been been

great great

friend friend

different different

# Word Cards: Words with *ee*

| wheel | sweet | bee | feet |
|---|---|---|---|
| she | deeds | he | sweeping |
| be | eve | agree | feed |
| beet | we | glee | tree |
| feel | flee | remix | these |
| extreme | delete | three | complete |
| theme | athlete | keep | green |

Unit 4 | Lend a Hand

# High Frequency Word Cards

| | |
|---|---|
| put | house |
| give | kind |
| does | place |
| away | both |
| before | been |
| after | great |
| through | friend |
| carry | different |

Name _____ Date _____

# Compare Settings and Plots

Use this comparison chart to compare the settings and plots of the two fables by Aesop.

| Title | Setting | Plot |
|---|---|---|
| "The Lion and the Mouse" | takes place in the forest | |
| "The Farmer and the Eagle" | | |

Share your comparison chart with a partner to talk about the fables.

**Phonics**

# Words with *ea*

Use paper fasteners and paper clips to make two spinners. Spin them both and use the letters to make words below. If the letters don't make a word, spin again.

> **Make Spinners**
> 1. Push a brad through the center of the spinner.
> 2. Open the brad on the back.
> 3. Hook a paper clip over the brad on the front to make a spinner.

**Beginning of word**          **End of word**

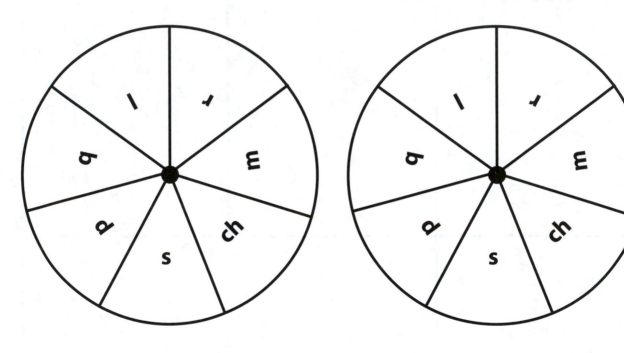

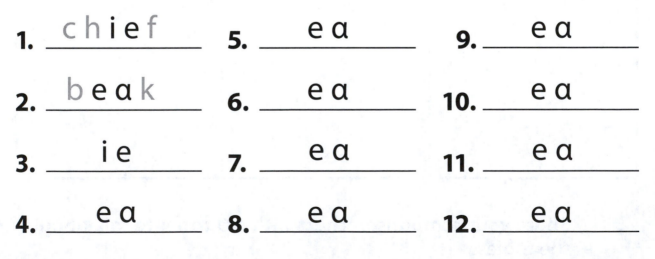

1. chief
2. beak
3. ie
4. ea

5. ea
6. ea
7. ea
8. ea

9. ea
10. ea
11. ea
12. ea

**High Frequency Words**

# Where Do You Live?

**Write a word from the box to complete each sentence.**

| High Frequency **Words** |
| --- |
| been |
| both |
| different |
| friend |
| great |
| house |
| kind |
| place |

**1.** Lee is my best _____.

**2.** We _____ live on the same street.

**3.** My house is _____ from Lee's house.

**4.** My _____ of house has three homes in it.

**5.** Have you _____ to my street?

**6.** It is a great _____ to live!

Grammar: Word Order

# Mix and Match Sentences

Choose words from each column and add any other words you need to make a statement. You may use words more than once.

| Naming Part | Verb | Object |
| --- | --- | --- |
| Mr. Yi | traded | fish |
| Mrs. Yi | caught | rice |
| Mr. Jia | shook | soup |
| They | dropped | bowl of rice |
| We | made | each other |
| I | paid | him |
| She | helped | it |

**Phonics**

# Words with *ea, ie*

Write the words to complete each sentence.

**1. beach   daydream**

Kim and Jess sit and _____ at the _____.

**2. sea   brief**

Then they go for a _____ swim in the _____.

**3. relief   heat**

It is a _____ to get out of the _____.

**4. seaweed   real**

Kim and Jess find _____ seashells and _____ in the sand.

**5. eat   peach**

Then they get a _____ and some peanuts to

_____.

**6. seagull   steals**

A _____ dives down and _____ some peanuts!

**7. sneaks   beak**

It grabs them with its _____ and _____ away.

**8. thief   scream**

Kim and Jess _____, "Stop that _____!"

---

For use with TE p. T228i              **PM4.24**              Unit 4 | Lend a Hand

Grammar and Writing

# Write Sentences

**Unscramble the words to make a correct sentence. Write the sentence. Use a period.**

**1.** need / help / I / with my homework / .

I need help with my homework.

**2.** helps / My brother / me / with science / .

_____

**3.** thank / my brother / I / .

_____

**4.** help / my brother / I / with the dishes / .

_____

**5.** each other / We / help / .

_____

Name _____  Date _____

# Use Sentences

1. **Play with a partner.**

2. **Toss a coin onto one of the sentence parts below.**

3. **Put it together with another sentence part to make a complete sentence.**

4. **Your partner takes a turn.**

5. **The player who makes the most complete sentences wins.**

| | |
|---|---|
| My friends | make good choices. |
| are thoughtful. | The teachers |
| My classmates | give to others. |
| help me study. | Mom and Dad |
| Our cousins | show respect. |

# Words with *oa, ow*

Circle the word that names the picture.

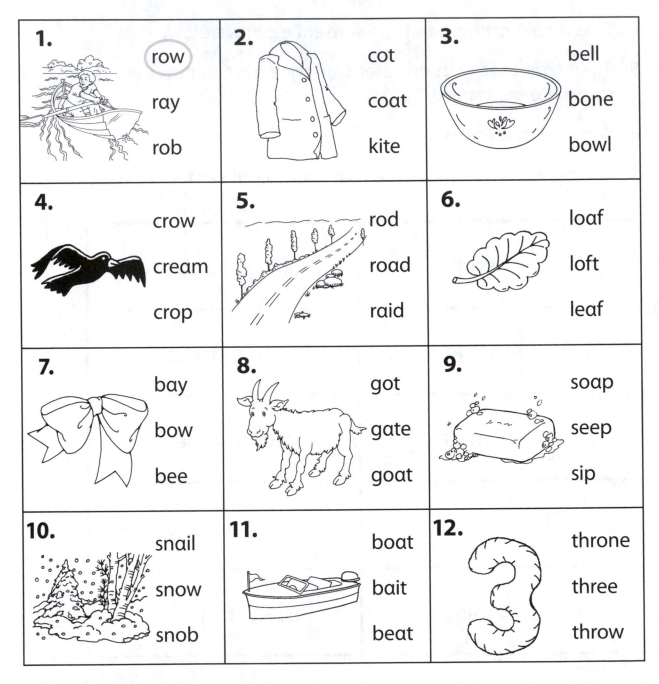

| 1. | row / ray / rob |
| 2. | cot / coat / kite |
| 3. | bell / bone / bowl |
| 4. | crow / cream / crop |
| 5. | rod / road / raid |
| 6. | loaf / loft / leaf |
| 7. | bay / bow / bee |
| 8. | got / gate / goat |
| 9. | soap / seep / sip |
| 10. | snail / snow / snob |
| 11. | boat / bait / beat |
| 12. | throne / three / throw |

**Read It Together**    I see a goat and a crow on the road.

Name _____ Date _____

# Sequence

Fill out the sequence chain to show events in order.

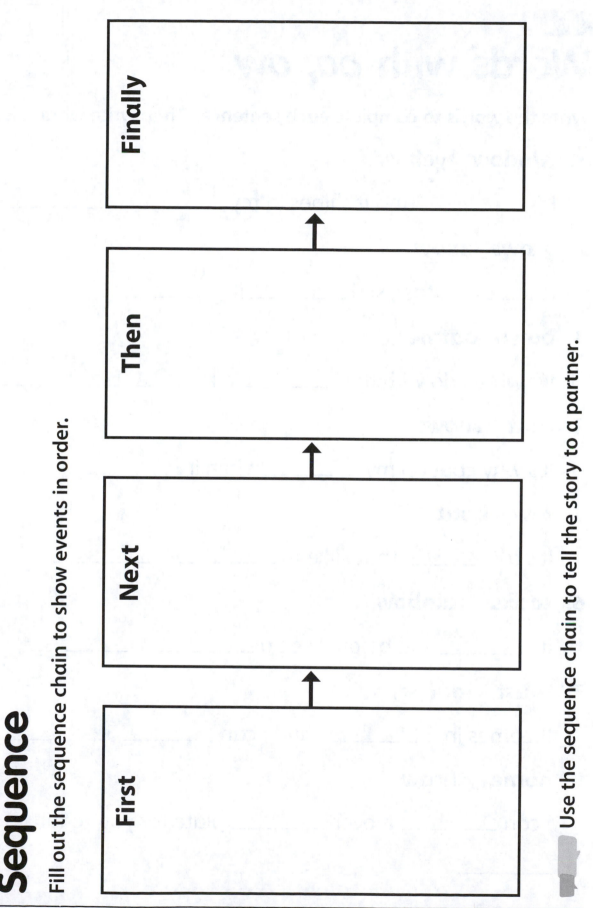

**First**

**Next**

**Then**

**Finally**

Use the sequence chain to tell the story to a partner.

For use with TE p. T231a

**PM4.28**

Unit 4 | Lend a Hand

**Phonics**

# Words with *oa, ow*

Write the words to complete each sentence. Then write what it is.

**1. window   yellow**

It's _____, and it shines in my _____.   _____

**2. grows   mow**

It _____ fast, so I _____ it.   _____

**3. bowl   oatmeal**

It's what I do with the _____ in my _____.   _____

**4. coat   snows**

It's why I put on my _____ when it _____.   _____

**5. row   boat**

It's a _____ that I like to _____.   _____

**6. soaks   rainbow**

It _____ me before I see a _____.   _____

**7. toast   loaf**

It comes in a _____, and I can _____ it.   _____

**8. home   throw**

I can _____ it over _____ plate for you to hit!

_____

**Handwriting**

# High Frequency Words

Trace each High Frequency Word and then write it.

may may

ever ever

nice nice

thank thank

push push

around around

teacher teacher

would would

For use with TE p. T232f    **PM4.30**    **Unit 4** | Lend a Hand

# Word Cards: Words with *oa, ow*

| | | | |
|---|---|---|---|
| boat | toad | window | elbow |
| bow | floating | toasted | swallow |
| throw | throat | mow | coast |
| moaning | narrow | goat | borrow |
| road | tow | groan | roadside |
| grow | row | steam-boat | below |
| moat | low | load | slow |

# High Frequency Word Cards

| | |
|---|---|
| off | may |
| going | ever |
| clean | nice |
| stop | thank |
| think | push |
| our | around |
| let | teacher |
| take | would |

Name _____  Date _____

# More Words with Long *o*

Complete the word to name the picture.

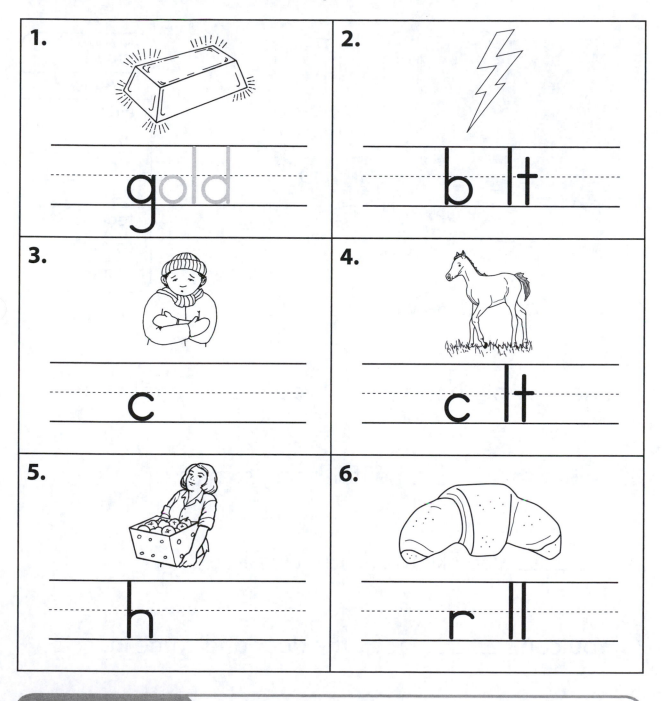

1. g**old**

2. b__lt

3. c__

4. c__lt

5. h__

6. r__ll

**Read It Together**   Can you hold a colt?

**High Frequency Words**

# Miss Gold

**Write a word from the box to complete each sentence.**

| **High Frequency** **Words** |
| --- |
| around |
| ever |
| may |
| nice |
| push |
| teacher |
| thank |
| would |

**1.** Miss Gold is a very nice _____.

**2.** She may be the best one I've _____ had!

**3.** I want to _____ her for being so nice.

**4.** _____ you like to see our class?

**5.** You can _____ open the door and come in.

**6.** Look _____. See what makes Miss Gold so nice!

# Word Cards: Subjects and Predicates

| | | | |
|---|---|---|---|
| the mountain | our hotel | you and I | those photographs |
| they | most people | a doctor | Alex and Connor |
| the mayor | her neighbors | children | sheep and cows |
| help | see | ask | want |
| hear | eat | visit | make |
| give | clean up | carry | show |
| remember | live | play | take |

Name _____ Date _____

# More Words with Long *o*

Write the word that completes each sentence.

**1. folding   strolling**

Jo is _____ down the path with her dog.

**2. gold   elbow**

Her dog looks _____ in the sunshine.

**3. window   old**

They pass an _____ gate.

**4. grow   colt**

A little _____ is with a man in the field.

**5. holding   soaps**

Jo is _____ her dog's leash.

**6. scold   both**

She uses _____ hands!

**7. don't   fold**

"I _____ want you to run through the gate and play!" she exclaims.

**8. strolling   told**

Now Jo and her dog are _____ back home.

**9. rolling   cold**

Jo is _____, so she wants some hot tea to drink.

# Write Subjects and Verbs

**Read the story. Then choose a word or words from the box that go with each sentence. Write the word.**

| the flyer | feel good because I helped a lot of people |
|-----------|---------------------------------------------|
| our home  | sometimes have trouble getting to the grocery store |
| I         | walked around on different floors |

_Our home_ is in a big apartment building. I decided

to help some older people in my building. They

_____ .

My dad and I _____ . _____

passed out a flyer with my name and phone number

on it. _____ said to call me and I would go to the

grocery store for them. Many neighbors used my

service. I _____ .

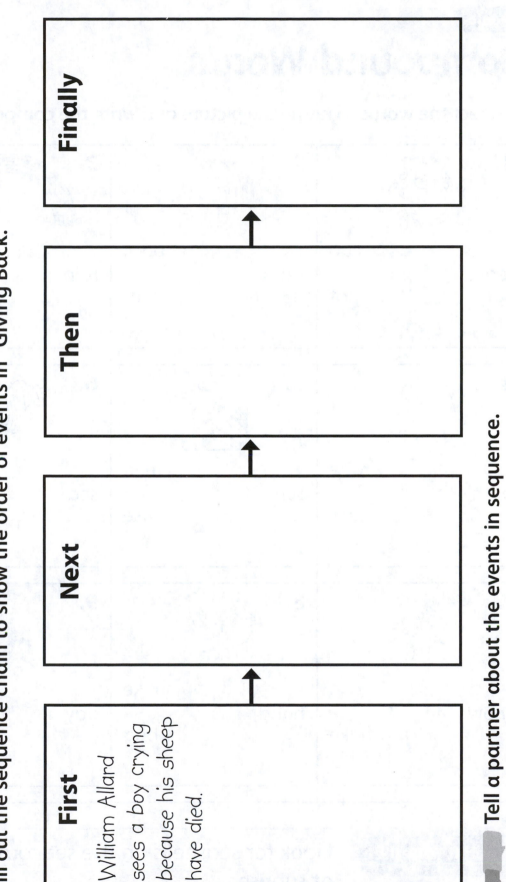

**Sequence Chain**

# Giving Back

Fill out the sequence chain to show the order of events in "Giving Back."

**First**

William Allard sees a boy crying because his sheep have died.

**Next**

**Then**

**Finally**

Tell a partner about the events in sequence.

Phonics

# Compound Words

Connect the words to name the picture and write the compound word.

**1.**
cup
tea ·················· pot
teapot
_____

**2.**
pack
back
seat
_____

**3.**
coat
rain
bow
_____

**4.**
robe
bath
tub
_____

**5.**
screen
sun
rise
_____

**6.**
coast
sea
shell
_____

**7.**
cap
snow
flake
_____

**8.**
shake
hand
bag
_____

**9.**
dream
day
time
_____

**Read It Together**  I look for seashells on the seacoast at sunrise.

**Phonics**

# Compound Words

Divide the syllables. Write the word that completes each sentence.

**1. sunshine   treetop**

The _____ was streaming in through the window.

**2. peanut   backpack**

Craig got his _____ and helmet to go for a bike ride.

**3. homemade   outside**

He went _____, but the day was gray.

**4. raindrops   weekdays**

Then some _____ fell on his nose.

**5. daydream   inside**

Craig went back _____.

**6. beehive   raincoat**

He put on his _____ and boots to go out and splash in the rain.

**7. sailboat   snowflake**

He went out, but a _____ fell on his nose!

**8. into   maybe**

Craig went back _____ the house for his hat and mittens.

**9. snowman   bedside**

Now he will go out to make a _____!

Name _____ Date _____

# High Frequency Words

Trace each High Frequency Word and then write it.

yes yes

say say

says says

write write

dear dear

name name

letter letter

answer answer

For use with TE p. T255b    **PM4.41**    **Unit 4** | Lend a Hand

# Word Cards: Compound Words

| | | | |
|---|---|---|---|
| newspaper | eyebrow | goldfish | rowboat |
| teammate | grownup | walking | blueberry |
| diagram | sandbox | ladybug | thermometer |
| watermelon | never | wheelchair | seldom |
| seaside | cookbook | scarecrow | table |
| dining | butterfly | sunshine | paper |
| campfire | tattoo | towels | footprint |

# High Frequency Word Cards

| | |
|---|---|
| land | yes |
| wash | say |
| city | write |
| much | dear |
| river | name |
| hold | letter |
| sea | says |
| mile | answer |

For use with TE p. T249g        **PM4.43**        **Unit 4** | Lend a Hand

Name _____ Date _____

# Compare Author's Purpose

**Work with a partner to fill in the comparison chart.**

| Author's Purpose | William Allard | Carol Jordan and Arwa Damon |
|---|---|---|
| to persuade | | |
| to inform | | ✓ |
| to entertain | | |
| to share experiences | ✓ | |
| to tell about other parts of the world | | |

**Which selection did you like best? Share your opinion with a partner.**

# Abbreviations

Cut out the cards and mix them up. Match the words to the abbreviations and use them in sentences.

| Mister | Mr. |
|--------|-----|
| Doctor | Dr. |
| Street | St. |
| Road | Rd. |
| Sunday | Sun. |
| April | Apr. |

**Phonics**

# Abbreviations

Monday → Mon.
Mark Joseph Smith → M. J. Smith

**Write the word that completes each sentence.**

**1. Mrs.    St.**

My mom is a teacher. Kids call her _____ Chan.

**2. Wed.    Mr.**

My dad is a teacher, too. He is _____ Chan.

**3. Dr.    Rd.**

Mom's class is going on a field trip
to see a vet. The vet is _____ Gray.

**4. St.    Sun.**

The kids get on the bus at 27 Pine _____ at 10 a.m.

**5. Oct.    Rd.**

They get off the bus at 9 Hancock _____ at 10:30.

**6. Nov.    Ms.**

They see the date Friday, _____10 on the vet's door.

**7. Mon.    P. C.**

The vet shows them Mr. _____ Mason's cat.

**8. Ave.    Feb.**

Mr. Mason and his cat live on Prescott _____ next to me!

**Grammar and Writing**

# Write Verbs That Agree

Read the story. Then choose a word from the box that correctly completes each sentence. Decide if you need to add *s* or *es* to the verb.

| feel | help | relax | take | wash | work |
|------|------|-------|------|------|------|

My mom is a hero to me. She ___works___ at a hard

job to support my brother and me. Sometimes she

_____ very tired after work and does not feel like

playing with us or fixing dinner. Then my brother

and I _____ as much as we can. We _____ the

dishes. My brother _____ out the trash. Finally, my

mom, my brother, and I all _____ .

**Grammar: Subject-Verb Agreement**

# Use Subject-Verb Agreement

## Grammar Rules Subject-Verb Agreement

Every sentence has two parts: the subject and the verb. The subject and verb must agree.

**The boy** wait**s**.

one person

**Parents** smile.

more than one person

1. Partner 1 points to a subject card.

2. Partner 2 points to a verb card.

3. If the subject and verb agree, cross out both cards.

4. Play until all the cards are crossed out.

| Subject Cards | | | |
|---|---|---|---|
| Avi | Teresa | Mr. and Mrs. Mendez | You and I |
| He | She | They | We |

| Verb Cards | | | |
|---|---|---|---|
| wants | builds | helps | hopes |
| work | study | need | carry |